The Modern Trusted Advisor

The Modern Trusted Advisor

Best Practices for High Value Executive Consultation

Nancy MacKay and Alan Weiss

BUSINESS EXPERT PRESS

Leader in applied, concise business books

The Modern Trusted Advisor:
Best Practices for High Value Executive Consultation

Cover design by Lisa Larter Group

Interior design by Exeter Premedia Services Private Ltd., Chennai, India

First published in 2021 by
Business Expert Press, LLC
222 East 46th Street, New York, NY 10017
www.businessexpertpress.com

ISBN-13: 978-1-63742-137-6 (paperback)
ISBN-13: 978-1-63742-138-3 (e-book)

Business Expert Press Human Resource Management
and Organizational Behavior Collection

Collection ISSN: 1946-5637 (print)
Collection ISSN: 1946-5645 (electronic)

First edition: 2021

10 9 8 7 6 5 4 3 2 1

Description

The best and the brightest use advisors and experts. In fact, one could say that they are the best and the brightest because they utilized trusted advisors throughout their careers.

Whether in business, sports, entertainment, academia, or politics, expert help is a fundamental enabler of success. That means that the demand for expert advice will grow, and the competition will increase for such help. This isn't a matter of "certificates" and "universities," it is a matter of specific skill and behavioral sets that create a trusting bond and reliance. Trusted advisors are beyond coaches—they are comprehensive resources and supporters.

The Modern Trusted Advisor employs important mastery traits, such as subordinating ego; applying shared experiences; and managing emotional, mental, and intellectual health. We are entering a world of "no normal" today, and leaders must inspire others daily.

This is the book that prepares you to inspire those leaders.

Keywords

advising; coaching; executive guidance; mastery; influence; executive success; strategy

Contents

Introduction

Our dream at MacKay CEO Forums and Summit Consulting Group, Inc. is to populate the world with inspiring leaders who, in turn, inspire and bring out the best in others.

We do this by partnering with inspiring trusted advisors who, in addition to their own successful private practice, deliver transformational peer learning groups for CEOs, other corporate executives, and business owners.

We have found that inspiring leaders and trusted advisors do three things particularly well:

1. Inspire themselves to take positive action every day, setting the example
2. Inspire people around them to take positive action
3. Commit to delivering extraordinary outcomes in all aspects of their lives every day

Our experience shows that the best performers in business, athletics, entertainment, politics, nonprofits, and other fields consistently use trusted advisors. It has never been lonelier at the top for CEOs and business owners, especially after Covid. Stress levels are high, inhibiting top performance. Stress (and guilt and fear) tend to "mask" talent.

As a trusted advisor, in order to inspire others to take positive action to speed up results, you need to inspire yourself to take positive action— you need to go first in a kind of "healthy selfishness."

What is needed is clear:
The future is about inspiring yourself to take positive action—you go first. If you skip this step, you won't be able to inspire your clients to take positive action and delivery extraordinary outcomes.

We have identified 10 areas of mastery to guide your journey.
Read on to learn how to help yourself to help others.

—Nancy MacKay, PhD
Vancouver, BC, Canada
December 2021

—Alan Weiss, PhD
East Greenwich, RI, USA
December 2021

Authors' note: Rather than engage in a cumbersome "Nancy" or "Alan" when relating personal experiences throughout this book, we have written it in the first person, combining our experiences. Henceforth, you will see "I" and "me" and "my" in the text, as well as "we."

CHAPTER 1

Time Mastery

You can always make another dollar, but you can't make another minute.

The Five Strategies: First, Take Control of Your Life

We have 365 days a year to maximize our lives and the lives of those around us. Executives often find themselves spending the preponderance of that time on business instead of family and instead of themselves.

As you can see in Figure 1.1, the "wheel of life" has eight components. None of these should surprise you. Evaluate yourself within these categories for familiarity, but then choose one of your clients or prospects and rate that person.

10 = Doing terrifically in these areas, more than ample time.
5 = Room for significant improvement.
1 = Hardly spending any time there at all.

Your (and your client's) maximum is 80 and minimum is 8. Our experience is that most people are somewhere around 50 to 70, but even those numbers are often overloaded and not equally disbursed (e.g., a 10 in career and money, a 1 in fun and health).

You may add other categories or change these, but the point is that you need a strategy for time mastery if you are to help those who see you as their trusted advisor.

You need to help your client make *choices*. Actors make choices all the time in how they will portray a character or react or move. Your clients don't always understand that they have these choices. We have to help them.

Taking control of your life also means that you understand what you can control and what you can't, and the reciprocity. You can't control the

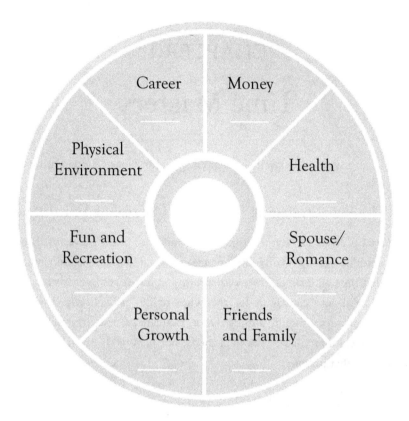

Figure 1.1   The wheel of life

Case Study Vignette

I was working with Felix the CEO of a 600 million dollar business, who was working 80 hours a week over six days a week. His wife was furious and demanded a change, and he was exhausted himself. We worked to reduce his time to 55 hours five days a week—these changes must be made in gradual steps—and he and his wife were overjoyed.

We not only improved his overall score on the wheel, but we also *reallocated* time so that he could reduce some time and money allocation and instead use the time on his spouse, family, and recreation.

Change can be gradual and be effective. Don't try to "flick a switch" from "off" to "on"; this is really a rheostat that needs adjusting.

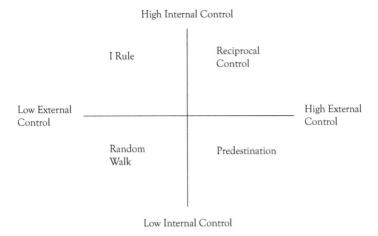

Figure 1.2 Locus of control

weather, but you can create rain dates or move an event indoors. You can't avoid taxes (and evading them is dangerous and illegal), but you can legally minimize them with expert's financial help.

You can see in Figure 1.2 that people who believe that there is neither external control nor internal control over their lives (bottom left) are simply taking a random walk every day. We sometimes find this with people who have inherited a business that they have not been prepared to run.

When people believe they have total control (upper left), they have the mistaken belief that they are unaffected by others and their environment, and have listened, perhaps, to so many motivational speakers. They feel that they rule their domains. We often find this belief in executives who have progressed through nepotism or blind luck instead of solid performance.

In the bottom right is total external control, with no influence at all from the individual. This is a kind of Calvinistic predeterminism that implies that it is senseless to challenge the fates. We see this often in leaders who have had very bad luck or been "outplayed" by the competition or who have been cheated or misled by people and institutions they trusted.

Finally, in the upper right are those who understand that they have control over many things, and there are many things that they can't control. They understand the reciprocity between the two. They are usually people who are resilient, pragmatic, and realistic. They don't expect constant sunshine, but they do know how to ride through bad weather successfully.

Winston Churchill said, "We build our houses and then they build us," referring to Parliament. But the same idea applies here. We create our lives and time allocation but then cannot be ruled by what evolves without our direct control and influence.

Keys:

- Help your client understand the allocation of time.
- Develop incremental ways to improve all aspects.
- Provide the accountability needed to ensure that action is taken and is permanent.

The Five Strategies: Second, Focus on Strengths

Have you noticed that most "self-help" books focus on weaknesses? They assume we were damaged and provide ways to "improve this" and "fix

---

Case Study Vignette

When I was fired, I had very little severance and very little in the way of savings. But I did have some major debts. I had to develop business as an independent consultant in a relative "hurry."

I quickly assessed what I was excellent at doing because:

- There is no learning curve.
- It isn't onerous to do what you like and do well.
- It can lead to instant (or very rapid) success.

I decided my strengths were writing and speaking. I loathed networking, didn't feel comfortable with "cold calls," and hadn't built up a network. So I wrote and spoke, spoke and wrote, everywhere I could, usually for free.

Leads began to arrive, some of which were from attractive buyers, some of whom met and hired me. Today, 60+ books and a thousand speeches later, I'm still writing and speaking. And you're reading this book.

---

that." However, we have found that the most powerful and executive leaders we have encountered in any field build on their own strengths.

According to a Gallup research study, only 17 to 30 percent of leaders do what they do best every day.[1] Most of your executive clients' time should be spent on applying their strengths on building, not on "fixing."

If you want to assess strengths, you can use tools such as the Clifton Strengths Assessment at gallupstrengthcenter.com or the tools provided by Marcus Buckingham at www.marcusbuckingham.com/invest-in-your-strengths-2/. Another top source is the Johnson O'Connor Research Center: www.jocrf.org.

Many of us don't realize what our strengths really are, hence the need for external assessments. However, we can also learn by soliciting feedback. Here is how you can do this, and here is how you can guide your clients through it:

- Make a list of your top 20 stakeholders, influencers, and empathetic friends and colleagues. Include clients, suppliers, professional services providers, board members, and so forth as appropriate.
- Ask what they perceive your strengths to be.
- Ask how you might apply them even better than you are.
- Ask for examples of situations and interactions where this advice would best pertain.
- Pack away your ego and just listen to the feedback, particularly patterns that emerge from disparate sources.

Your passion plus your competence plus others' needs will provide extraordinary results. However:

- If you have passion and competence but no need, you have a message no one wants to hear.
- If you have passion and need but no competence, you won't be able to help (and will lose to the competition).
- If you have competence and need but not passion, you merely have a nine-to-five job.

[1] Roth, T., and B. Conchie. 2008. *Strength Based Leadership, Great Leaders, Teams, and Why People Follow: Gallup.*

Case Study Vignette

Greta had recently completed a high-profile acquisition that was a game changer for her business and the highlight of her career. However, instead of basking in the limelight, it was sucking the life out of her and she was contemplating selling.

Encouraged to take the CliftonStrengths assessment, she identified her strengths to be: Strategic, Achiever, Learner, Relator, and Self-assurance. She then asked key stakeholders for feedback on her strengths and opportunities for improvement. Through this process, she realized that dealing with the media, which was taking up half of her time, was not a strength. She had taken a lot of media training but was never going to be masterful in this area.

She developed a 90-day plan to minimize her time spent on PR, hiring a Vice President of Communications to take over most of her media-related duties. She now spends less than 20 percent of her time in this area and 80 percent of her time in her areas of strength: setting strategy, doing deals, leading her team, and building relationships with strategic customers.

What are your top five work-related activities? These have the largest impact on your performance and, therefore, your organization's performance. How would you assess your current ability in these areas?

Masterful: Extraordinary, unparalleled.
Excellent: Superior to most, consistent.
Competent: Adequate, but not passionately involved.
Peripheral: Sometimes fail, stressed, uninterested.

Adjust your schedule, activities, and delegation to spend more than 80 percent of your time on your Masterful and Excellent activities. Outsource everything else.

Achieving time mastery isn't so much about finding time to do more things as it is *focusing solely on the right things to do.* We often take on tasks for these deadly reasons:

- We feel we can do them better than others.
- We are doing someone else's "failure work."
- We enjoy doing them.
- We are in a rush.
- We don't delegate well.

Ruthlessly focusing on your strengths and continuing to build them will enable your clients to achieve what seems like miraculous improvements in a very brief time.

The Five Strategies: Third, Eliminate Ego Talk

The "ego" is that part of the mind that alternates between the conscious and subconscious and determines self-confidence, self-esteem, and self-worth.

There is a profound difference between efficacy and self-esteem. Efficacy denotes how well you can do something. I can write and speak well, but I cannot play an instrument and can barely play the radio. We are not efficacious at all things. *We need to be efficacious about our calling and our passion.*

Self-esteem is about our sense of worth *irrespective of our efficacy.* Even if I err in something, I should be effective in doing (e.g., I make a poor speech) that doesn't mean I'm less of a person. The problem in time mastery is that so many executives' self-worth calibrated to their last victory or defeat!

In Figure 1.3, you can see the relationship.

Upper left: Healthy, constant self-worth can absorb the vicissitudes of life and work.

Lower left: An "empty suit" who exhibits huge self-esteem but isn't efficacious. (In Texas, known as "big hat, not cattle.")

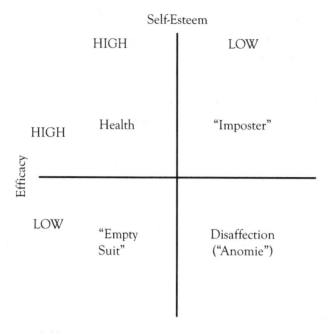

Figure 1.3 Self-esteem and efficacy

Case Study Vignette

Lorraine was a new CEO who had delivered extraordinary business results in her first year and was very pleased with her year one accomplishments. Her only disappointment was the 30 percent of her time spent fighting with and complaining about her board. She described them as micromanaging dinosaurs and wanted advice on how to get them off her back. 360-degree feedback uncovered a huge surprise—her board was about to fire her!

Working with a board-appointed coach, the CEO stepped into their shoes and realized that they were all successful business leaders who were doing their best to get her set up for success. She stopped getting defensive at board meetings, stopped complaining about her board to her management team, and apologized to her board. She learned how to park her ego and instead show up as a leader with both the board and the management team—just in time.

Upper right: The imposter who has high efficacy but doesn't feel good about it and believes he or she will be "found out." (Actors are often in this area because even when they win an award, it is for portraying another person, not for themselves.)

Bottom right: The person who is alienated from society and feels neither accomplished nor worthy. (There is a type of suicide known as "anomic.")

How much time do you or your clients spend trying to look good, avoiding accountability, and undermining others, as oppose to taking accountability, sharing credit, and supporting others? Behaviors that enabled someone to reach a certain point are hard to give up. Thus, inappropriate and harmful behaviors that nevertheless achieved prior success are often still employed, even though unnecessary or even destructive.

Too much time is wasted on propping up egos, and, counterintuitively, we all save time by sharing and applying our energies only to the results we need to accomplish in our careers. It is amazing how many consultants, coaches, and trusted advisors often begin dealing with a prospective client as if he or she must be the "problem," that they are somehow "damaged."

How many of those people choose the same approaches with their people—employees, colleagues, stakeholders, customers, and investors?

Here is a comparison to think about in terms of whether you are more concerned about looking good (ego) or truly leading (crediting and supporting others):

Ask your client in terms of the time they are investing:

- Is it for blaming or taking accountability?
- Is it for judging or showing respect?
- Is it for defensiveness and accepting and considering feedback?
- Is it for an insistence on being right or valuing others' perspectives?

These answers and progress toward the house of leadership not only maximize mastery of time but also provide for productive, healthy organizations. In Figure 1.4 below you'll see the difference between merely looking and helping others look good.

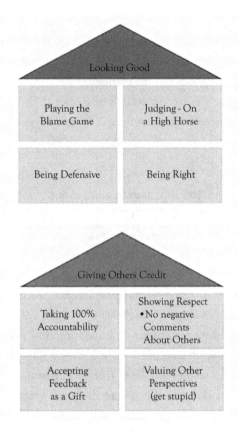

Figure 1.4 Houses of ego and leadership

The Five Strategies: Fourth, Create and Practice Mental Toughness

A great deal of time is wasted over two major issues:

- Having a tough time making tough decisions
- Procrastination

These are related, of course. Our definition of procrastination, which is born out of fear is this:

Procrastination is the fear of the critique or a finished product, a decision, or an initiative that is greater than the fear of being critiqued for not doing it at all.

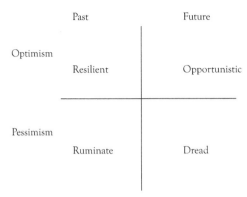

Figure 1.5 Optimism and pessimism

This is not a condition conducive to strong leadership, and it is one that trusted advisors must be alert to and help to resolve.

In a world of hypercompetition, advanced technology, disruptive influences, and market volatility, it is tough to feel as if you're "in control." The antidote for this is mental toughness.

We probably have 100,000 ideas and thoughts travel through our minds daily, 90 percent of which are irrelevant or banal or unmemorable. It is also easy for us to focus on the negative and threatening as opposed to the positive and optimistic.

Herein is the profound difference. As you can see in Figure 1.5, our choices are to be resilient about past errors and opportunistic and positive about the future, as opposed to ruminating about the past imperfections and dreading more mistakes in the future. All of this is about mindset and a tougher mental attitude.

We need to enable our clients to focus above the horizontal line *all of the time*. This is where better decisions are made, where productivity is optimal, and where we make consistent progress toward corporate and personal goals. *The vehicle moves in the directions that one is looking.*

Action steps:

- Evaluate your own mental toughness. How much time do you spend, realistically, above and below that line?
- Develop the "triggers" and self-awareness (or even external help—see the following Case Study Vignette) to realize you have dipped below the line and move upwards.

- Minimize your "beat yourself up" time over past mistakes. We recommend 60 seconds.
- Gratitude is the opposite of fear and loathing. Try this exercise: Every morning, first thing, remind yourself of three positive things you'll accomplish that day, personal, and/or professional. Every evening, remind yourself of three things that you did accomplish well, no matter how major or minor. Help your subconscious cleanse your head.

Never be afraid to use others to help you as a "gyroscope" to keep your mental toughness upright and functioning. Also use the proper rationale. One example: Many leaders have a tough time firing people. They worry about repercussions, their image, the other person's family, and so forth. But the fact is firing someone is the kindest thing you can do when they simply can't perform in a job after you have done your best to help them. That's how to understand the tough decision is the best decision.

Case Study Vignette

An established CEO with a track record of success decided that he wanted to quit and help his owner bring in a turnaround CEO. Jerry was convinced that the business was going to fail under his watch. He had just lost his biggest customer, his bottom line had taken a big hit from U.S. dollar rate changes, and his CFO had "screwed up the numbers."

He showed up at his peer group meeting overwhelmed by anxiety and the weight of self-blame. One of his peers asked him, "If you knew you couldn't fail, what would you do?" He said he would do a deal with his biggest competitor, fire his CFO, and work with his leadership team to develop a 90-day turnaround plan.

His peers helped him get "above the line" and get the nonsense out of his head so he could focus on success and the compelling vision he had to be the industry leader. He left the meeting with a 90-day plan to turn the company around and is still running the company, now recognized as a "Best Managed Company" today.

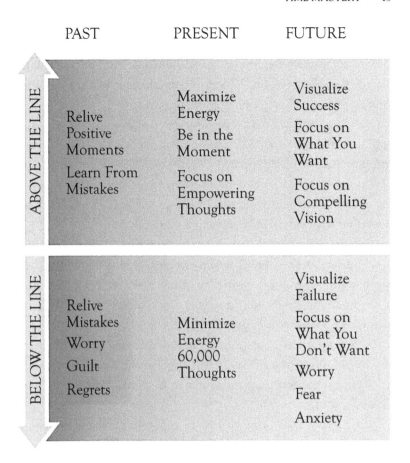

Figure 1.6 Mental toughness success habits

Your clients, no matter how high and mighty, need reinforcement and help with this if they are to master time.

Figure 1.6 shows a more detailed way to look "above and below" the line for mental toughness. We only deal in three dimensions, but can only take action in the present. So we can spend our present time neither regretting the past nor dreading the future. We all have only 100 percent of our energy and time to allocate.

The question is: Where do we place it for success?

The Five Strategies: Fifth, Apply the Happiness Formula

When I coach executives, the first question I ask is "Are you having fun?" The reactions are pretty much those of astonishment, with the explicit or implicit response, "I'm not supposed to be having fun!"

Have you been around people who are naturally upbeat and happy, optimistic and opportunistic? Have you noticed that this kind of energy and enthusiasm is contagious and seems to spread to the group?

Leaders waste too much time diverting their energy to being miserable and trying to figure out how not to be (or whom to blame). But there is relief for this. We call it The Happiness Formula.

Dan Gilbert, the rock star of psychology currently Harvard's chair of that department, wrote *Stumbling on Happiness* (Knopf 2006).[2] He explained to me over scotch in Cambridge that "synthetic happiness" is as important as genuine happiness. The latter includes birthdays, births, anniversaries, winning a prize, getting a promotion, and so forth. But the latter occurs when you hear people say, "Breaking my arm turned out to be a gift" or "My illness actually woke me up to life" or "Getting fired was the best thing that ever happened to me" (and, for me, it was).

His research shows that people are happy in groups or communities. People who said they believed in God were no happier on average than those who said they did not. But people who said they attended church were happier on survey than those who did not. *Happiness is about community, kinship, and connecting.*

Thus, back to The Happiness Formula:

LC = Life Condition
E = Expectation
If LC = E, then that's great.
If LC ≠ E, then Houston, we have a problem.

---

[2] Another excellent resource is *You Can Be Happy No Matter What: Five Principles for Keeping Life in Perspective*, Dr. Richard Carlson (New World Library, 2006).

Case Study Vignette

The country president of a global company was very unhappy when he didn't get his sought-after promotion to become the Global CEO. The board had appointed a female CEO, and Larry was convinced that the decision was gender-based rather than merit-based. He played the blame game—the board members were all idiots, the recruiting firm was incompetent, and his executive coach was useless. He was ready to resign.

His coach convinced him to map out his options using The Happiness Formula. There were at least three options to change his life condition—stay, quit, and negotiate an expanded role. There were also at least three options to change his expectations—accept this as a learning opportunity that will help him be better prepared to get the role next time, park his ego and accept that all the stakeholders did their best and made a difficult choice, and admit that he wasn't ready yet for the Global CEO role and welcome the opportunity to compete for the role again in the future. He opted to change his expectations and stay in his current role. Three years later, Larry became the Global CEO, turned the company around, and is still running the company today.

The point about happiness is once again, control (see Figure 1.2). You can change your conditions and/or your expectations. The importance of taking control is that you have only 100 percent of your energy and time to apply to anything, personal and professional. When people say, "Give me 110 percent," it is a nice motivational saying, but it means exactly nothing pragmatically.

How much of your time and energy is organized around internal worry and strife as opposed to external accomplishment and results—impact on the environment around you? This is the question to broach to your advisory clients. Figure 1.7 shows the distinctions of internal and external focus. What are your percentages?

The best leaders we have worked with address 90 percent of their efforts and resources toward their accountabilities, relationships,

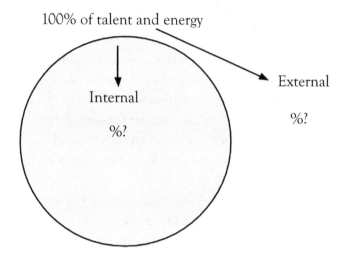

Figure 1.7 Internal versus external energy deployment

customers, employees, stakeholders, and so forth. But only about 10 percent is directed toward stress, strife, resolving unhappiness, and inn conflicts. (When this number goes way up, the individual can't be "coached out of it," but therapeutic intervention is needed.) However, even a 50/50 split seriously undermines effectiveness and damages self-worth, as well.

Hence, our job is to improve the happiness quotient of our advisory clients, and we would better improve our own, first. We create the contagion of happiness with them, and then they do so with their colleagues, staff, and families. Consider it a "positive pandemic."

Chapter Return on Investment

- "Managing time" is insufficient, we must master it.
- Time is not a resource, it's a priority, so the key is how we allocate it and reallocate it.
- Focus on building strengths, not correcting weaknesses.
- Use assessments to uncover hidden strengths.
- Passion + competence + need = extraordinary results, but you can't get by with two out of three.
- Efficacy and self-worth are independent variables.

- Be careful and positive with your self-talk.
- Isolate negative experiences but generalize positive ones.
- Don't be "ego-vulnerable."
- Practice mental toughness.
- Stay "above the line" in dealing with the past, present, and future positively.
- Remember The Happiness Formula. People deserve to have fun and enjoy their careers, exercising control to ensure their mastery of them.

CHAPTER 2

Ego Mastery

Ego definition: The part of the mind that mediates between the conscious and the unconscious and is responsible for reality testing and a sense of personal identity.

Ego as a Game-Changer or Show-Stopper

"Ego" is a neutral term. It refers to a mental and emotional state of being. Our egos can propel us forward or bring us to a shattering stop. There is nothing wrong with what people call a "strong ego." In fact, most excellent leaders with whom we have worked have strong egos. That doesn't mean that they are arrogant or bullying or imperious. It does mean that they have a strong sense of self and, to use the standard test, are comfortable in their own skin.

As trusted advisors, it is important to:

- Have our own egos under control, so that we do not, inadvertently, become entangled in competitive dynamics with clients or feel threatened by them.
- Help our client control their own egos, which are usually strong, so that they are powerful and productive and not dysfunctional and undermining.

Ego mastery, therefore, isn't about subordinating ego so much as applying it appropriately and situationally.

All of us need to "look good." We want to be liked, and we want respect. But these aren't synonymous. This may seem jarring, but respect is far more important than affection in this work. It is helpful if people like us, but it is far more important that people respect us. I may like you, but I think you are giving me poor advice or poor direction. But if I

Case Study Vignette

One of my clients, Rick, was a brilliant CEO, one of the best I have ever encountered. However, I noticed that at the meeting of his executive team, he constantly cut people off and finished sentences for them.

When I pointed this out, he admitted that he did it, but said, "I want to move the meeting along. I know what they are about to say, and I can summarize it more quickly and save time."

"Maybe," I responded, "but you are not allowing them to take credit for their thinking and their contributions. They believe that you don't respect their opinions or that they don't express them well. What does another 30 seconds really cost you?"

He agreed to change, I taught him to count in his head "one thousand one, one thousand two" when someone else took a breath to ensure that they were finished speaking. This changed the entire tenor of the meetings. Rick's ego wasn't out of control, but it needed some subordinating at times.

---

respect you, I'm going to be much more prone to listen to and implement your suggestions and direction.

I don't need to like the heart surgeon or the intellectual property attorney or the winning Super Bowl coach. I want to work with, play for, and trust the people who I respect.

In Figure 2.1, you will see that low respect and low affection simply make you a "vender." We have all been in the position at times in our careers where HR simply sees us as venders, no different from a computer salesperson or someone peddling office supplies. In the bottom right, we are a "buddy." We were liked but not necessarily respected. I enjoy watching the game with you or going to dinner, but I would never ask you for advice.

In the upper left is the converse, I don't feel at all close to you but I recognize your expertise. This is the "expert witness" testifying on the correct procedure for the implementation of heart stents.

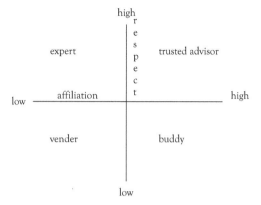

Figure 2.1 Respect and affection

In the upper right, we have the true trusted advisor. Affection and respect are not synonymous, but they coalesce here in someone who is trusted and relied upon.

Your ego and your client's ego are both adjusted so that you are not "judging" or defensive or blaming. You are not on your "high horse" and neither is the client. Being a trusted advisor is about collaboration and synergy, not combat and competition! It is not about being right, it is about being helpful. In other words, if you are trying to prevent your client from cutting other people off in mid-sentence, don't cut your client off!

You need to subordinate your own ego to allow feedback to be effective, and this is why the upper right quadrant in the diagram is so important. Consider this "ego continuum":

Intimidated	withdrawn	participative leading	directive overbearing arrogant

A "strong" and healthy ego is not in the right, but somewhere in the middle. (Note that "bullying" is not on the chart because bullies have very low self-esteem, and try to bully people down to their own levels of perceived inadequacy. This is a personality disorder, not an ego issue.)

Many people are so defensive about themselves that they become offensive, striking out at others before they can be (in their perception) struck. We have found that the more aggressive people are, the more insecure they are. Assertiveness and confidence are positive traits.

Let us conclude here with these definitions:

Confidence: The sincere belief that you have the ability to help others.
Arrogance: The sincere belief that you do not need any help for yourself.
Smugness: Arrogance without the talent.

Self-Awareness

The key to "parking" one's ego is to be self-aware, especially when we find ourselves in a negative emotional state, for example, angry, annoyed, frustrated, outraged, and so forth. When this happens, here is what you (and your advisory client) *should not* do:

- Pick up the phone and call someone to vent.
- Write an e-mail to vent.
- Sit around "stewing" about it.
- Plan retribution.

Instead, recognize these dangerous and destructive triggers and move into a positive emotional state. That might seem easier said than done, but if you can be self-aware of these indicators, you can redirect yourself and certainly serve in that capacity for your clients.

Ask yourself what true success would look like.

What if you did nothing, would the situation get worse, stay the way it is, or decline and abate?

Will action on your part exacerbate the situation?

Will what you are considering be unretractable and nonrevokable? You can always change a poor setting on equipment, but you can't "unring" a bell or erase what you have said to someone.

Too many of our ego-driven thoughts are negative. We have a propensity to focus on defeat, setback, failure, and perceived inadequacies. We don't sufficiently focus on victory, triumph, accomplishment, learning,

Case Study Vignette

The CEO, George, was disappointed with his bonus after a good year and felt his overall package was beneath those of peers in the industry. He said to his wife, "The board chair is a jerk, he's jealous of me, and I'm going to quit to show him he won't be able to make it without me."

His wife tells him to talk to the chair and express his disappointment, not anger, and he can still quit after that if he wants to. He says to him, "I'm vastly disappointed, to the point that I'm considering leaving, and I wanted to pay you the respect of telling you that face-to-face."

The board chair replied, "I think your evaluation was fair, but I don't want you to be unhappy with it, so why don't we convene an independent third-party committee to review your performance and your overall compensation?"

That improved the CEO's condition immediately. The committee eventually did not recommend that he receives a larger bonus but did recommend that his incentives be changed to be less ambiguous and more valuable the next year.

He is still with the company and highly productive.

and growth. We need to help our clients to focus *on what we can control and move forward.* People tend to overuse the word "authentic," but we think it means owning our own feelings and being accountable, understanding the impact of your actions on others, and being honest about what we need versus what we want.

Humility is not degrading ourselves, but understanding the worth of others and appreciating that worth.

Have you experienced people who stop at the bottom of a moving escalator to figure out which direction to go? Or have you seen people leaving a crowded theater who stop in the exit doors to discuss the show? I was with a group of six people at a top restaurant that didn't take reservations for six but graciously allowed one for us because our hotel concierge requested it. When we arrive and were seated, one of my party, in this jammed place, asked the hostess if we could have better table with a view.

These aren't necessarily malicious people, just marvelously unself-aware. We sometimes call them "clueless," which is an unfortunate pejorative, because we should be helping our clients (and ourselves) to be more sensitive to others and the environment at any given time. I have heard obscenities at business meetings uttered by people who normally use that language with some of their clients without a problem, but it becomes a problem when they don't compensate for the group they are now with.

Here are some techniques for self-awareness to test on yourself and to suggest to your advisor clients:

- Do you consider the people you will be with and the environment in which you will be, or do you only consider your own comments, needs, and results?
- Do you listen carefully to questions and comments, or do you regard them as interruptions?
- Do you observe nonverbal behavior and expressions as you are speaking?
- Do you "test for understanding" and ask questions to see if people are following you, that your pace is effective, and that your points are understood?
- Do you allow others to be the "host" or facilitator and take a "back seat" role when appropriate, not trying to dominate conversation?
- Are you able to patiently engage in conversation and the interests of others even if not within your own interests?

Move yourself to "conscious competency" from "unconscious competency." We generally don't think about how to tie a shoe or put on a piece of jewelry. But we can't really learn unless we move to conscious competency. (I have to open the clasp and insert the other side.) This is vital for improving our self-awareness.

We can't simply assume that others view us and our actions in the same way that we do. What matters are the other peoples' perceptions because perception *is* reality.

Mastering Emotions

Emotions have become more valuable for people to understand and manage recently. The approaches of EQ (emotional intelligence) have been popularized by Daniel Coleman, among others. We are talking about the capacity to be aware of, control, and express one's emotions, and to handle interpersonal relationships judiciously and empathetically.

Empathy is the ability to feel what someone else feels (as opposed to sympathy, which is feeling pity or sorrow for others' plight). To practice empathy—to be empathic—we have to rein in our own emotions, especially when serving as a trusted advisor.

Remember that logic makes people think, but it is emotion that urges action. We may think something is a great idea but not take action on it for years. Many of us have faced buyers who seem to agree with everything we have said about our ability to be of help but never sign the contract. We have played intellectual chess with them but not emotional rugby.

Thus, *urgency*, the overarching feeling to take action, comes from the emotions, not the intellect. You don't see a fire approaching you and run because you decide it is the rational thing to do. You run immediately sensing that there is an urgent need to escape danger.

Why is this so important in advising others? Ask yourself some of these questions.

- Can you recognize when you are in an intensely emotional state? This is part of the self-awareness discussed earlier. The negative side of emotions urging us to act is that emotions can be triggered inappropriately or at the wrong times. Can you recognize the difference?
- Can you move yourself from a negative state to a positive state without others' intervention? That is, can you control your emotions or do they control you?

- Do you recognize that you are not always in the right emotional state to make an important decision? This may come from recent traumatic events or people you dislike involved or too many obligations facing you. Some people talk about "flow" or bio-rhythms being important. (Remember the advisories after certain medications "not to operate heavy equipment"? I have always wondered if their definition of "heavy" and mine were the same!)
- Am I well rested with a healthy diet so that I'm in the best physical shape to make decisions and not allow physical discomfort to affect my emotional state?
- Are your stress levels sufficiently low and controlled so that you aren't readily "triggered" into rash behavior?
- Do you have the "courage of your talent" in that you seek respect, not primarily affection, and you can tolerate being disliked or resented, knowing that you are doing your best in the best interests of your clients?

Now, this may have been the easy part! Helping ourselves is within our control, and we can solicit coaching if needed. But how do you help your client, who may be resentful or completely misinformed by his or her people? How do you part *other* people's egos?

We recommend an MVE approach:

Mirror what you have seen or heard.
Validate the other's feelings.
Empathize and feel what they feel.

MVE is about acknowledging your client's feelings (I understand that you are upset about your bonus amount), validating the point of view (It makes sense to be disappointed given what you have told me), and empathizing (If I were in your shoes, I'd be disappointed too).

This is how you "talk people down" from overly emotional states. Note in the case study vignette my advice to my son to make a rational, logical, decision (take a subordinate role) not a visceral one (boycott the play). What happens to you is often very emotional, but what you do about it has to be logical and pragmatic.

Case Study Vignette

My son was in his senior year in the drama department at the University of Miami. The big production was going to be John Steinbeck's *The Grapes of Wrath*, and Jason had clearly put in the work and received the notices to be eligible for the lead, Tom Joad.

We received a call at the house and Jason told my wife, "Let me speak to Dad." Now, when your kid asks to speak to Dad you know it's *never* good news! He told me he was passed up for the part and that the theater department actually brought in someone from the outside for the role.

"How do you feel?" I asked.

"I feel betrayed, furious, frustrated, outraged, hurt, and very sad."

"And why are you calling me?"

"I want to know how I should feel."

"The way you feel is the way you feel. I'd feel the same. There are not 'right or wrong' feelings."

There was an exhalation of breath.

"But," I continued, "I know what you may be thinking. You may boycott the play, tell your friends not to go, appeal to the dean—or—take a subordinate part, and do a great job."

He took the subordinate part and was terrific, and he confessed later that he wasn't right for Tom Joad. *It's not what happens to you, it's what you do about it.*

Your clients will often miss that distinction. It is our job to practice this differentiation ourselves to the point we become adept at helping others to immediately master emotions by placing them in the right context at the right time.

The Fine Art of Feedback

There are varied reactions to feedback. One of my colleagues says, "The only thing you can do with feedback is listen to it." But it implies that you should also feel free to ignore it.

There is a difference between *solicited* and *unsolicited* feedback:

- Solicited: Comes from a trusted source whom you respect and who you have asked for comment.
- Unsolicited: Comes unrequested from anyone.

Unsolicited feedback is nearly always for the *sender*. It is an attempt to try to "equalize" by providing "help" that is actually a statement that the sender knows more than you or can perform better than you. I remember a woman in Philadelphia who belonged to the same speakers association that I did who would *always* seek me out immediately after a speech and tell me that she disagreed with me, or I could have done something better, or "here is the way I do it."

This isn't about being polite, it is about avoiding the fate of becoming a ball in a pachinko machine, constantly battered by bumpers and flippers as it is pulled down by gravity! "Recency confirmation" is the tendency to believe what you have most recently heard at the expense of earlier—and, perhaps—wiser advice. Hence, the admonition, "Give the boss your thoughts right before the meeting begins and you'll have the most influence."

As an advisor, park your ego and don't tell people what to do. As a rule, a therapist will never offer you strong advice but will generally prod and question, and ask what you intend to do, or how you feel. Rather, share your own experiences to create empathy and talk about your own "hits and misses." Then encourage your client to do the same.

Imagine the difference with your advisory client when stating the second comment rather than the first:

- The problem is that you used poor judgment and acted too rashly.
- Let me tell you what happened to me when I thought speed was more important than being certain.

The second reaction embraces the other person is a common circumstance, while the first is a dictate from a superior position. Shared experiences are a great way to give feedback, and as a trusted advisor, your

Case Study Vignette

Jenny was a coaching client who always tried to position herself as "the second smartest person in the room." No matter whom she was with, she would offer commentary. She would try to change the agenda before others' meeting started, often even suggest different restaurants and social activities for the groups.

She was forever running overtime during his presentations. Even when told publicly that she had 10 minutes left, she would sail on for 30 more (remember "lack of self-awareness"?). Jenny couldn't always be the leader, but she figured that she could always be the second most important, "the second smartest person in the room."

The only way to get this feedback across to her was with a confrontation during a session where she was running seriously beyond her time. She left the room in a huff. But later, she asked for help from the people she respected, the true "smartest people in the room."

Sometimes it takes "tough love" to provide feedback that will be heeded.

power is in providing such experiences from a wider client base and larger frame of reference. Sharing, rather than *telling*, is the strongest way to provide feedback that others will accept.

As a trusted advisor, your feedback is always "solicited."

We should request feedback from those we respect, and advise our clients to do so, as well, not just from us but from others in their business and personal communities. Once you can discriminate between solicited and unsolicited feedback and between trusted sources and other sources, you have a "litmus test" that enables you to utilize effective and well-intended feedback.[1]

Ego will get in the way of receiving feedback, hence, the need to "park" ego elsewhere. We need to open ourselves up to improve and that means allowing for vulnerability.

---

[1] Some "unsolicited" feedback can originate with trusted sources who have decided that they can give you help even if unasked.

I call this "The Lobster Principle."

No one really knows how large lobsters can grow or how long they can live. There was an 80-pound lobster pulled up (and returned) and another that was thought to be 100 years old. (There is a kind of clam called a "quahog" that grows in chilly waters off New England and into the Arctic, and living examples have been found believed to be 500 years old.)

A lobster has an exoskeleton—a shell. That shell must be shed (molted) if it is to grow. When that occurs, the lobster is vulnerable to predators and seeks shelter. However, this process is perpetual, and eventually the lobster grows too large even for its predators, so long as it can successfully grow its new shell.

We need that vulnerability if we are to grow and that ability to allow for critique and "tough love" without resenting it or being hurt. The greatest leaders—and the greatest advisors—we have ever observed allow for that vulnerability.

Chapter Return on Investment

- We don't grow by playing a "blame game": search for cause, not blame.
- Maintain a positive emotional state.
- Practice empathy more than sympathy.
- Use the MVE method to deal with emotional issues.
- Don't tell people how you would do it, explain how they can do it.
- Use shared experiences rather than critique.
- Not all feedbacks are valid or deserve consideration.
- To accept legitimate feedback, we must agree to be vulnerable.
- Your ego state has to be constant, not dependent on your last victory or defeat.
- Self-awareness is critical, and we need triggers to remind us to be self-aware.
- We have to dedicate 90 percent of our thoughts to the positive and productive, not fear or dread.
- Logic enables us to think, but emotions urge us to act.

CHAPTER 3

Shared Experience Mastery

Who's in Their Shoes?

We discussed in the last chapter how important it is to engage in feedback that utilizes shared experiences. This creates a trust and a bond that "cements" the ability to accept feedback and change behavior. Obviously, this will differ depending on your advisory client, and places a high premium on your being able to involve yourself in diverse experiences and circumstances.

It is always amused me that a dozen of people from the same local chapter attending a national convention will opt to have dinner with each other—which they can do year-round—rather than meet new people and dine with them! There is also this comic observation about "the other guy's shoes":

To walk in someone's shoes, rise early, take their shoes, and walk for at least a mile. That way, when they awaken and realize their shoes are gone, you'll have a good head start.

Your clients are going to have experiences that include these elements of their lives and professions:

- Work environment
- Work content
- Hierarchical role
- Travels for business
- Travels for pleasure
- Family or lack of family
- Health and fitness
- Recreation
- Entertainment
- Civic involvement or noninvolvement

- Hobbies and interests
- Philanthropy
- Professional associations
- Aspirations and expectations

You don't need, obviously, to relate in all these areas. (I don't have too much to say to someone who plays the cello in spare time other than "Isn't that Yo Yo Ma terrific?") Just a few of these areas will suffice.

If we engage in listening 80 percent of the time, we will learn about many of these areas. The more we talk, the less time and opportunity there is to learn. Don't be in a rush to always get to business issues. Take the time to listen for comments in these other areas with which you may be able to form shared experience.

Sharing experiences should be judgment-free and nonprojecting. "Projection" is the human tendency to assign our own traits—successes and failures—to others. "You won't be able to ski the blue hills your first time out, so be content with the green hills first." That's uttered by someone who couldn't handle the harder hills the first time and assumes you can't either. People want to tell me all the time how tough it is for them and will be for me to write a book, after I have written 60+!

So we don't pass judgments or project. Instead, we listen and empathize.

Case Study Vignette

I was beginning my career at Prudential and made a pretty ghastly mistake in copying a policyholder on what should have been strictly an internal, confidential document.

My manager, Bob, sat down with me and made sure I understood the proper procedure, very calmly and patiently. Then he said, "You know, I was about your age when I actually approved a $25,000 claim that never should have been paid and we could never recover. I expected my boss to fire me. But she said, 'I have just invested $25,000 in your training, so you are too valuable to let go now!'"

I have tried to emulate that approach ever since.

Telling people what to do turns most people off, and egomaniacally telling them how you do things better will drive them crazy. And remember in advising anyone: You have accountability but no authority. THEY have *both* accountability and authority over their people. So, while they can exert reward and punishment as accountability tools with their authority, you need a different approach.

Hence, shared experiences help you to create great empathy and agreed-upon new directions.

We often use a two-minute share experience drill during small group meetings in preparing trusted advisors. We call this ISAR:

Issue: What is the issue to be resolved?
Situation: What is the surrounding involvement of people and the environment?
Action: What is the best intervention?
Result: What do we wish to achieve and are we successful?

We now have the opportunity to master shared experiences in these categories.

If the issue is to improve presentation skills in large group meetings, what have we experienced that lend a common basis to the discussion?
If the environment is one of skepticism and distrust, where have we encountered it and what do we recognize as important to consider?
If the action is to involve everyone in questions and answers, what are our learnings in what works and doesn't?
If the results intended are for consensus and the agreement to give things more time, what have we experienced that convinces people to concur with this request?

The question of who is wearing whose shoes is more than a metaphor. It is incumbent upon advisors to create as many shared experiences and recollections as possible to create the mentality of "walking through this together." One you master that and demonstrate it through your actions you enable your client to do so with his or her people, as well.

The wider your experiential base, the easier it is to recall and create shared experiences.

The Drama of It All

Here is an exercise that fosters the power of shared experiences:

- Create a time and place
- Create a realistic character
- Create a surprise or dramatic event
- Make a business point in a nonjudgmental way

Example:

- It is a Friday afternoon during a financial firms busy (tax) season.
- The CEO of the firm is being torn by the need to guide some people late into the evening about deadlines that can't be missed, and a promise made to attend the daughter's musical recital that evening.
- The spouse suddenly calls the CEO's cell phone to remind about the evening plans, and there is panic about the conflict. If you were there somehow observing, what would you advise?
- The CEO asks the spouse, "I need your advice. Here is the situation that I'm facing, and, frankly, I'm torn because this business is paying for those musical recitals. The spouse says, "She will be crushed if you are not there.

The point here is about life priorities. There is only one musical recital like this, and the daughter will never be 12 years old again. There is really no option to "make up" or atone for missing this. But on the work side:

- The CEO can choose two trusted aids to oversee the work.
- The CEO can come in over the weekend to make up for any crucial lost time and sign-offs.
- Deadlines can often be extended.
- You can accept a penalty if you must for missing a deadline.

In the future, it is probably more important to look at preventive action for such frantic last-minute pressures, such as better staffing, longer deadlines, and more confident delegation.

So the issue here is one of understanding *all* of the ramifications and creating sane and sound options. The more we have experienced such conditions—*or have counseled others in such conditions*—the more we have shared experiences of high credibility and pragmatic responses.

Telling people what to do is the default position for many executives. They believe that they are paid to take action. But here is the key for trusted advisors:

Executives are NOT paid to take action; they are paid to achieve results.

Case Study Vignette

Terry, the CEO, was attending a meeting of his top people and realized that his CFO, Norm, should be fired because his responses were slow and sometimes not completely accurate. The banks were making noises about credit and loans because reporting deadlines were being missed or information supplied to them wasn't complete.

The CEO thought that he could "roll up his sleeves" and get the job done with Norm removed until a replacement could be found, perhaps also utilizing the director of finance in more high-level work.

I advised the CEO that one of my other clients had attempted the same thing. The director turned out to be over her head with the higher-level information and was also not cleared for some delicate matters. The company controller was also weak—not at all in the succession plan—and the CEO just couldn't handle everything. The answer would have been to retain the CFO with more careful monitoring and accountability until the current crisis passed and a decision could be made about a replacement, from within or without.

Terry said, "I hadn't even thought of those possibilities and repercussions." Despite being urged by other subordinates to summarily replace Norm, he waited and hired a replacement three months later after current deadlines were met.

Sometimes those results are based on *inaction*, which is often seen as counterintuitive and not dramatic enough, but is, nonetheless, exactly what is needed. Yet most "advice" emanating from colleagues and subordinates (and many consultants) is to "do something, now, show that you are in charge." That has often failed business leaders, presidents and prime ministers, university heads, and nonprofit directors.

It is the trusted advisor's key role to present positive and successful shared experiences—or *un*successful and negative shared experiences—in order to direct the client to success and results.

We often hear sports commentators remark after a poor play or decision, "He would like to take that pass back," or "She probably regrets that kick." You can't take an athletic play "back" and you can't unring the bell of a business decision. Shared experiences from the past are the preventive for negative experiences in the present.

Obviously, the "drama" we are talking about her in shared experiences is a form of storytelling. Stories, whether spoken or written, are primarily methods to transfer *value* to others. They are effective because others like to hear stories to which they can relate and with which they can identify. Sharing experiences via stories allow for learning from the experiences of others, good and bad. They remove the pressure of trying to prove that we are the smartest people in the room and need to retain that status by telling people what to do.

When we use stories to learn, we join a "group" of peers and problem solving and decision making become much easier because they are "supported" by those peers.

A hint to advisors on stories:

I keep a "story log" using software (I use FilemakerPro, but you can also use a simple spreadsheet). I keep a keyword for each of the stories I want to retain for possible use in the future. In other words, "open gate" would represent my story about my dogs running through an open gate and not pausing to do a risk analysis. If my client had dogs, the client will immediately understand the shared experience and will be amenable to listening to the dangers of being too conservative.

Keep a story log and you will always have a "reserved" of shared experiences to use in a dramatic fashion to gain commitment. My memory is otherwise not that great and, when I counted up my totals, I had 126 stories, growing weekly!

Mining the Client's Experiences

Clients have their own "story log" but they just don't realize it.

Shared experience mastery means just that: sharing. But how do you "mine" the richness of the other person's background?

Let us say that the other person mentions a tennis championship as they're speaking: "It was right after the tennis championship that I learned…."

You intervene with:

"Excuse me, but what championship was that?"

"Sorry to interrupt, but were you in that championship?"

"Just a moment, please, but when was this, what year?"

"I have to stop you: How did you get involved in a tennis championship?"

You are polite, but you are not letting the moment go. When you say something like, "Excuse me, may I interrupt?" that is what we call a "rhetorical permission." In other words, the other person can't object ("No, you may not interrupt me!"), but you are being polite about the request. The problem is that we are often so busy thinking of our own next lines, our own stories, or own responses, so that we miss the significance of what the other party is saying.

The reason for the aforementioned "story log" is to ensure that we don't "lose" valuable lessons. Since the people we were advising usually will not have such a story log, they are apt to mention casually and randomly things that we really ought to make note of.

After all, everyone has a story to tell.

A friend of mine who dabbles in fiction begins every conversation with a new acquaintance with "What is your story?" He is generally interested in the response. And he focuses on what is said, often asking people to stop and dig deeper into a story or experience. I copied that topic for myself.

You should be asking your clients:

- Why was that notable?
- How did you feel when that occurred?
- What is the chronology of events leading up to that?

Case Study Vignette

I was at the American Press Institute delivering a workshop on story use for editors of a variety of newspapers.[1] I was emphasizing the exact points that I'm making in this chapter.

A woman sitting near the rear of the amphitheater reported that, in her team, she couldn't produce anything because her life was vanilla and uninteresting. Here is the conversation that ensued:

Me: Well, where did you go to school?

Her: West Point.

Me: West Point?! (I calculated quickly in my head.) You must have been among the first classes to admit women.

Her: It was the very first class with women.

Me: Well, how did that turn out for you?

Her: I was student body commander.

Me: Isn't that the highest rank a student can hold?

Her: Yes.

Me: And what happened after graduation?

Her: Not much, I went into the army.

Me: What branch?

Her: Paratroops.

Me: Paratroops?!

Her: Yes, I volunteered.

By now, the entire room was fascinated and laughing. She saw her story as simply her history, nothing special. The rest of us saw this as amazing.

Epilog: Many years later, she wrote me, having followed my books and newsletters. She had become a Carmelite Nun! We still exchange Christmas Cards!

---

[1] Alan is the sole nonjournalist in history to have been granted a Lifetime Achievement Award by the American Press Institute.

- What did you learn from that?
- How do you use or apply this today?
- How can you use this in your current position?
- Have you considered sharing this with others?
- Has this happened often?

Mastering shared experiences requires that you help your client to recognize and share his or her "story log" and build on those stories and experiences to enrich the advisory experience.

Chapter Return on Investment

- Success is about listening not telling.
- Park your ego, it is not about you and your experiences solely.
- Utilize the issue/situation/action/result approach (ISAR).
- Utilize the "drama" of time/place, character, surprise/drama, business points.
- Focus on positive actions from experiences.
- We learn through focusing on experiences and stories.
- Keep your own "story log."
- Mine the "story log" of others.
- Never try to be the smartest person in the room.
- Don't be afraid to interrupt to focus on key experiences.
- Ask, "What's your story?" to learn more, especially with new clients.

CHAPTER 4

Social Contribution Mastery

Give back to your community through volunteer commitments and make the world a more inspiring world for all human beings (desperate need at this time).

The Beneficial Organization

I was fortunate to work for Merck Pharmaceuticals for 12 years as an external consultant. During that time, they won Fortune Magazine's poll as "The Most Admired Company in America" five times. (I don't claim credit, but they were smart enough to use my help!)

The prevailing aphorism within Merck (which is not associated with the German pharma company of the same name) was by the founder George Merck: Do good, and good will follow. This was in the company's annual reports and its domestic literature but also within most people's hearts at the time. No one joined Merck to get rich, as they might with a Wall Street private equity company or selling real estate. They joined because they identified with the vision and value of the company: "We bring the greatest in scientific research to the greatest areas of human health need."[1]

What George Merck was talking about was that if you do the right thing as often as you can, you will do just fine on the bottom line. As of this writing, Merck is #69 on the Fortune list, and the 52nd most valuable company in the world at about $200 billion.

Nancy's company, MacKay CEO Forums, was certified as a B (beneficial) Company in 2018, one of only 300 in Canada and 3,000 in the world because of how they treat their employees, commitment to

---

[1] As I'm writing this, in an unprecedented move, Merck has agreed to produce Johnson and Johnson's Covid vaccine.

sponsoring charities, commitment to diversity, and inclusion of 1,200 CEOs around the world in mutually supportive groups. This inspires new members to join, creates "evergreen" members of those who do join, and also motivates members to qualify their own companies as a B Company.

Since Covid, thousands of firms around the world are applying because they want to demonstrate that business is a force for good, for positive change, and just what George Merck was talking about. As a trusted advisor, this is what you can suggest to your clients and help them accomplish.

This is what we mean by "social contribution mastery."

Alan has designed a new approach to strategy, Sentient Strategy®, that looks forward no longer than a year and can be formulated in a single day by owners and executives. Its two prime factors are:

- Impact on the environment
- Awareness of the impact of your decisions and actions

This is meant to accommodate and reward social contributions. Peter Drucker famously pointed out:

An organization is not like a tulip or a cheetah, successful merely by dint of perpetuating the species. An organization is successful in terms of its contribution to the environment.

If you can demonstrate these characteristics, you can then serve as the exemplar for your clients. Are you:

- Taking a stand on important causes
- Confronting inappropriate behavior and language
- Combating harassment and bias
- Demonstrating that we must take the time to "do good"
- Coach, mentor, and share with others without remuneration

Merck was trying to develop a drug at one point that was unsuccessful in trials. But they found out accidentally that the drug completely cured African River Blindness, which was at the time the top killer in Africa. No one there could afford the drug, so Merck donated it to whomever needed it.

Case Study Vignette

I was waiting at my veterinarian to pay a bill and glanced at the Merck Manual open on his desk. When he returned, I said, "Merck is one of my largest clients."

The vet, Dr. Marcetti, became glassy-eyed and said, "Are you aware they have done more for the well-being and health of animals than any other company in history?"

By coincidence, I had a speaking engagement two weeks later for Merck's (then) animal health division. I related that story and there was dead quiet in the room. I was stunned.

I asked the vice president later if I had said something inappropriate.

"No," he said, it is just that they constantly hear about later deliveries, errors in the product mix, and so forth. They don't hear the great stuff we do."

Then maybe you should have some vets on this stage or send your people to their offices," I suggested.

Today, African River Blindness has been eradicated.

Covid has undermined business support for many good causes. In the arts, for example, corporate contributions have all but stopped, so that regional theaters, dance, and music have had to rely on individual donors, government stimulus, or go into debt. Many have had to shut their doors. This is even more crucial with institutions trying to help youth, disadvantaged families, and the mentally ill.

The most outstanding leaders of these organizations don't allow a scarcity mentality to intrude. They remain positive and seek to marshal help. They reach out to others. Strong leaders in private enterprise have to respond. The must do good so good will follow.

We are not talking about public support for political parties or for the most recent "flavor of the month." We are talking about being responsible citizens of the community—and the community includes the neighborhood but is not confined to it in a remote and digital age. An organization is a citizen of the world and must act accordingly. No organization can

---

Case Study Vignette

The CEO, Dennis, said that he simply didn't have the time to provide the chairmanship of the local United Way campaign, see his daughter in the school music recital, and run his company 60 hours a week during the busy season. He rationalized that his job supported his United Way financial contributions and his daughter's school, so work had to come "first" and required most of his time.

However, I pointed out that time is not a resource but really a priority. He has the same time every day, and it is up to him how he allocates it. When he says that he doesn't have time to see his daughter, that is untrue. He does have the time *but chooses to allocate it to other things.* Why not choose to allocate it to the recital, which is only a single night, and delegate things at work to others because the issues will still be there tomorrow.[1]

We "cop-out" when we simply try to throw money at problems. Our chairing a charity committee or appearing at a school event can be of far higher impact than simply writing a check, *nor are they mutually exclusive.*

---

simply "take" (money, market share, land, resources, talent). The finest organizations "give."

Are you serving on boards of directors? Are you encouraging your clients to do so? On private boards, you can influence this kind of benevolent thinking, and on nonprofit boards, you can share your expertise.

The Social/Business Nexus

We don't operate in isolation. We, as trusted advisors, and our clients, as business owners or executives, are members of varying communities. There is our physical location, where we should be good local citizens,

---

[2] By the way, when a prospective buyer tells you that she doesn't have the time for something, use the same reasoning. She does have the time, and she merely needs to reallocate some of it to you.

obeying the laws, supporting civic efforts, sponsoring local improvements, and participating in events. This might include sponsoring a youth soccer team, attending zoning board meetings, supporting certain political candidates, volunteering for government post (e.g., board of education), joining the chamber of commerce, and supporting the local arts groups.

We are members of our professional communities, locally, nationally, and perhaps, globally. This would include attending events, serving as mentors, contributing to publications, serving on panels, serving on boards, and sharing best practices.

There is no "line" between business and communities. They are synergistic, and they should support each other.

As individuals, we should be putting our resources and expertise "on the line" to assist others. We have served positions on the board of Blueprint to build more inclusive communities; on the board of the Elizabeth Buffam Chase House, a shelter for battered women, to combat domestic abuse; on the board of governors of Harvard University's Center for Mental Health and the Media.

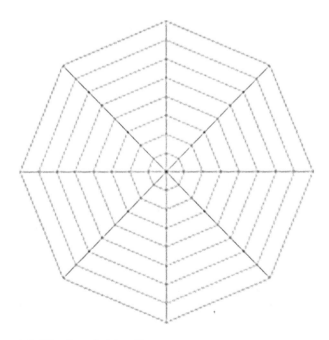

Figure 4.1 The "good citizen"

These efforts are not *competitive* with the time we need on our jobs and in our professions. They are *supportive* in that they help us all to become more well-rounded and productive people.

We all need to evaluate our efforts in being solid citizens of our communities, as business leaders and as people. The spider chart in Figure 4.1 gives you the opportunity to evaluate your own "good citizenship."

Starting at "12 noon" assign each of the main axes a value, such as:

- Community volunteer
- Active in charity fund raising
- Support of local arts
- Belong to professional organizations
- Serve as mentor/coach
- Support political candidates
- Provide best practices to the profession
- Keep abreast of local events through news and groups

Now give yourself a "10" if you believe you're doing this thoroughly and well on any point (place this on the perimeter) and a "0" if you don't do it at all (place this in the center), or a number in between the center and the rim.

How do you appear? Not many of us would be consistently on the outside, but some of us are consistently in the center. We need to focus ourselves and our clients on a more well-rounded social/business nexus.

An "inspired leadership 'you go first' strategy" is a roadmap we've created and utilize with clients to inspire themselves to inspire others. That's where ratings like those above are useful. Many of us, and many of our clients, are simply too busy to be aware of these social needs and "obligations." Our clients need to be directed to them. Most or the excuses, when these issues are raised, are, "I don't have the time." Of course they have the time, and we have to help them to reallocate it.

This is part of the scarcity mentality which haunts many leaders. Most of their advice comes from financial experts and advisors. They so are constantly worried about their businesses that they, themselves, don't have enough money. Hence, they spend a great deal of time making sure they have "enough," but "enough" turns out never to really be enough!

I asked a group of business owners not long ago what they would do with a $600,000 windfall they didn't expect and was theirs, free and clear. None would spend all of it. Some would reinvest in their business while taking some time for vacations. Some allocated varying amounts to charity and good causes.

But I'll never forget one woman, who was more successful than she ever dreamed she would be and who was in the midst of her best year, ever.

"I wouldn't touch a penny of it!!" she yelled.

The Watertight Doors

Social contribution mastery must be based on our own growth. Our lives are not snapshots but are movies, constantly in motion and changing. We tend to think tomorrow will be like today, but it never is. As Tevye sings in Fiddler on the Rood in the song "Sunrise, Sunset": "I don't remember growing older, when did they?"[3]

Change has to be conscious and "mastered." That is, we need to change deliberately as we mature and grow. Values, beliefs, and perspective that stood us in good stead years ago may well no longer be valid in maturing lives. To help others to change in our capacity of advisors, we have to change ourselves.

It's always interested me that in going to high school class reunions some of the "kids" have changed considerably—not just in age, but in demeanor, language, lifestyle, interpersonal skills—but *most have not changed at all.* They have the same biases and baloney they had in high school except now with grey, thinning, dyed, or bald heads. It staggered me when I realized that so many were "stuck" in an eternal time warp.

As I moved into advisory work, I found myself having to develop an archetype of change (or lack of change) so that people could relate and identify where they are. We too often still think of ourselves as the kids arguing over who owns the ball or who should be first in line. I chose to call the sequence "the watertight doors" because I believe we have to "seal" the doors behind us in order not to slide back.

---

[3] Bock and Harnick (1964).

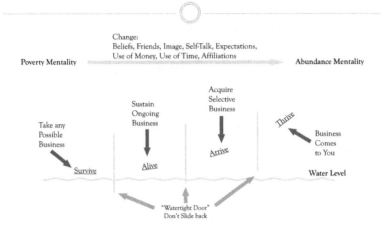

Figure 4.2 The watertight doors

Watertight doors require progressing from a scarcity and poverty mentality to an abundance mentality, as seen in Figure 4.2. On the left is *survival*, new to a business or a position, where we are trying to make a go of it. We will take on any business as an entrepreneur or any assignment as a manager. We need to put bread on the table. This is a time when we are not at all discriminating.

We move to the right, if we are successful, to *alive*. We can sustain our own business here or hold our own on corporate turf. There may not be much in reserve and we have to be extremely flexible and hardworking, but we do have some security and credibility.

Success there brings us to *arrive*. At this level, we have created a sustaining, growing business and can be selective in our acquisition of clients. Our brand is becoming stronger.

This leads us to the *thrive* level, where customers and clients come to us. Instead of asking, "What can you do for me?" prospects ask, "How can we work together?" You are considered a thought leader and your brand is very strong. Perhaps you "own" the niche in which you thrive.

In terms of social contribution mastery, we are now in a position to engage more easily and with higher impact with social and political issues, with fairness and with developing others. We have stated earlier that wealth is discretionary time. At the thrive level, we have that time to invest in a variety of important activities.

However, the watertight doors must be sealed and kept firmly shut. As we move from survive to thrive, we are also moving, left to right, from a scarcity (poverty) mentality to an abundance mentality *presumably*. But for many people, that mental shift doesn't occur.

We are not talking merely about money, picking up a check, or making a charitable contribution. We are talking about:

- Sharing information
- Providing time
- Providing expertise and coaching
- Providing resources (space, staff, supplies)
- Stimulating creativity and innovation
- Making introductions
- Providing referrals and business leads

We all know many people who, while apparently highly successful, won't share a thing with anyone, won't provide help, are ready to sue people for presumed incursions into their business or intellectual property, who are hugely defensive and will never admit to a mistake.

Those are not exactly the hallmarks of an "abundant mentality."

Look at the very top of the chart and you will find that the movement from scarcity to abundance and the ability to seal the watertight doors relies on making *changes in yourself*. You have to examine and often change your beliefs, friends, professional colleagues, memberships, subscriptions, image, brand, expectations, time investments, and financial investments. Without changing these beliefs and habits, how on earth can we move from poverty to abundance?

We can't.

Social contribution mastery, for you and your advisory clients, requires that we develop the intent and ability to apply ourselves for the good of others. That means that we have to have the attitude of success (thriving) and the confidence that we have moved from our early days and tough starts (scarcity) to our current state of success and achievement (abundance).

Our beliefs and self-talk inform our behaviors, which are manifestations of our beliefs. Our behaviors inform others of who we are and how they can expect us to act.

Alignment

I was asked by a local dance company to run a strategy session and I found that the vice president of the organization didn't have a season subscription and felt no need to purchase one. I asked the president of the board, privately, why they didn't throw him out.

Social contribution master often overlaps with business necessity. When the American Institute of Architects asked me to set strategy, I found they had a board of 54 people, totally unwieldy! But their intent was to embrace the widest possibility of interest groups within the organization, from solo practitioners to huge firms, and from commercial to residential. We solve the strategy issue by naming an executive committee of just 12 members empowered to set strategy with the others' input.

Social mastery exists within organizations. You can influence and even command people through:

- Hierarchical power: Using one's position and authority to require change, as in the military. You don't sit down and have a consensus session when the colonel gives an order.
- Reward and punishment: People have the ability to provide incentives or disincentives, such as preferential work assignments, overtime pay, too much or desired travel, and so forth. Someone in a lower position in human resources can often dole out or withhold benefits and resources.
- Expertise: People often follow those whom they are sure are "in the know" and can be trusted for their mastery of the subject. The top sales producer is a valued mentor because that person has the ideal track record of success. We often call this "social proof."[4]

---

[4] This is the "ski instructor phenomenon." Do you want an instructor sitting in the lodge sipping brandy and telling you what to do in the morning or someone who is with you in the morning, six yards in front going down the slope, demonstrating what has to be done? And remember that no one ever learned to ski by reading a book.

- Referent: This is often called "charismatic" but that is too much of a bland stereotype. We are talking here about someone who is trusted, who instills confidence and belief, and who people readily follow *irrespective* of the possession or nonpossession of the preceding bullet point traits.

Alignment includes the passion we spoke about earlier. So many people we meet can't seem to find what they have to offer. Yet we all have those items from the progression through the watertight doors to offer: resiliency, change, adaptability, optimism, refusal to slide back, and willingness to help others to improve.

Ask yourself, whether in business or social settings, does this align with my "calling"—my purpose in life—and can I offer significant help? Does it fill me with gratitude and elation?

It is not about money. Alignment is never about money. People use excuses such as not enough money in order *not* to commit. There is an old and useful observation about charity: The amount of money you give is not as much an indicator of generosity as the amount of money you have *left after you give*.

Thus, alignment is about the synergy of your beliefs and values, your business intent, and your ability to help others. Marshall Goldsmith is probably the greatest executive coach in the world[5] and here is how he states his mission in every newsletter:

> *My mission is simple. I want to help successful people achieve positive, lasting change in behavior; for themselves, their people, and their teams. I want to help you make your life a little better. Thank you for subscribing! Life is good.*

A successful trusted advisor provides the example as well as the advice and encouragement for creating social mastery as part of one's life, including the business experience. We all socialize (and did so even during the Pandemic, remotely) at work as well as at leisure. To be effective, we need

---

[5] He and Alan coauthored. 2017. *Lifestorming: Creating Meaning and Achievement in Your Career and Life*. Wiley.

to create effective relationships, interventions, and movement toward (and sustaining) an abundance mentality.

Chapter Return on Investment

- Become involved in the community, charities, causes, and support groups.
- Take a stand on what matters.
- It is not just about money. Provide time, resources, information, moral support, emotional support, and so forth.
- Move to the right and sustain your abundance mentality, eschewing a scarcity or poverty mentality.
- Slam shut and secure the watertight doors.
- Understand and act on the fact that there is a huge social mastery approach even within businesses and organizations.
- Become a "beneficial corporation" (BC).
- Remember that you must exemplify these conditions that are important for your advisory clients to embrace and master.

CHAPTER 5

Innovation Mastery

Innovation is not something left to teams, committees, or special "skunk works" in remote buildings. It is rather about incremental improvement every day and is one of the most profound approaches to leadership success in any business.

Typology

Problem solving is about fixing things that have gone wrong in the past. A person, a process, or a piece of equipment is not performing in the manner it should and has deviated from the expectation and from past performance. In the most cases, it must be "fixed," though in some cases, it is replaced (or fired).

Innovation is the establishment of new and higher standards and the achievement of new expectations. It is created today, and the results are in the future—in five minutes, tomorrow, or next year. It is far riskier than problem solving because in problem solving, we *know that the expectations can be met and were being met—the thing used to work!* With innovation we have a risk that the new "bar" may not be met and we may even suffer some adverse consequences from having tried to reach it.

There are three types of innovation that not everyone realizes and are vital for us to know as trusted advisors:

Opportunism

This occurs when someone is "triggered" by an event or experience and can take advantage of it. We hear "opportunistic" as an adjective of merit, although sometimes pejorative ("He was too opportunistic seeking the promotion").

Case Study Vignette

There was a power outage in my town, and the local Dunkin' Donut's coffee shop couldn't open. Yet people unaware of the outage were still heading there for their morning coffee and donuts.

A man pulled into the lot with a canteen truck, the kind that caters breakfasts to plants and office buildings. He started selling his inventory and was sold out within an hour. No harm, no foul, people were happy with the substitute and Dunkin' didn't "lose" any business.

This is opportunism. The problem is that many people never examine what is around them for opportunity.

Synthetic happiness ("Being fired was really a blessing") is rife for opportunity. During the pandemic, some people used the time to build new, remote businesses; to learn to play a musical instrument; to paint; to read books they have always wanted to read; to write a book they have always wanted to write.

Others simply stewed in their own juices, bemoaning their fate.

Conformist Innovation

This occurs when you improve an existing circumstance, and it is very common. Uber is nothing more than an improvement over age-old taxi services but with ride hailing, GPS, clean cars, fluent drivers, and a better environment. (Which is why taxi companies have had to clean up their acts with drivers who are not on the phone, not eating lunch, actually can find addresses, and are polite.)

When someone decides to improve the way in which a customer complaint is handled or decrease costs in shipping, these can be examples of conformist (and incremental) innovation.

Nonconformist Innovation

Welcome to Amazon (and what has been called the "Amazonification" of the business world). There is nothing that Amazon is replacing or improving upon, it is a new phenomenon.

To dramatize this, once upon a time Sears and Roebuck were non-conformist innovators, using the new, late 19th century transcontinental railroads to deliver catalogs to widely diverse settlements in the West. People ordered by return trains, and goods were shipped, from foods to prefab houses, from furniture to tools.

So why didn't Sears naturally morph into Amazon?

Because Sears successive management focused on profit and the brick-and-mortar empire they had created and not innovation. Sears is bankrupt today, Amazon is a global giant, and its founder, Jeff Bezos, is the richest man in the world.[1]

Segway inventor Dan Kamen is a highly successful entrepreneur, but his vision for a single motive device for people is used today only by some tour operators, warehouse owners, and police forces. It flopped as a commercial endeavor. As I said, innovation has risks.

Case Study Vignette

Harley Davidson has had the most profound motorcycle brand in the world. However, its demographic is consistently older, they have not attracted younger riders. They recently closed their entire Indian operation because their bikes are too big for the roads and too expensive. Yet India has 17 percent of the entire world's population.

In the United States, they have tried to hang on to their aging customers by producing "trikes," three-wheeled vehicles for people who are too old and obese to straddle a traditional bike.

Why didn't Harley go into the ubiquitous scooter market, where powered scooters are for rent in every large city controlled by smart phones for charging batteries and finding the nearest vehicle? Because Harley stopped innovating a long time ago.

Like its typical customer, it hasn't aged gracefully despite its one-time dominant brand.

---

[1] And that is after giving his first wife *$35 billion* in a divorce settlement that makes her the 22nd richest person in the world today!

We have to assist our clients in utilizing all three forms of innovation, in their personal lives and professions and businesses. We all tend to get into the "rut," as in cross-country skiing, a rut someone else has made. And that is just not as exciting as a good downhill run.

Real Innovation in a Virtual World

Innovation will help your advisory clients as much or more than any other process and discipline. We have tended to regard "disruption" and "volatility" as negatives, but they present opportunity. In fact, the best organizations have used disruption and volatility as offensive weapons. Alan introduced value-based fees for consultants (which should be the basis for your advisory retainers) in the 1990s, and he has the strongest independent consulting brand in the world today.

Whether you are dealing with clients in person or virtually, the key for you and them is to surround yourself with innovatively-minded people. For example, in Nancy's community, over 60 advisors meet monthly for an hour or more to exchange new ideas, novel methods, and thought leadership approaches. You clients should be using you as well as others in those roles for themselves.

A "speed dating" approach involves lightning-fast questions and answers that two people can use to generate great ideas rapidly. In just 30 minutes, rapid questioning coupled with generosity and sharing can produce scores of new ideas. This is a great exercise for trusted advisors among themselves, or to implement within client companies. Just present a need or idea and see, quickly, what the other person can add to it or how they can help with it.

We all need "game changers" who come with great ideas and the assertiveness and confidence to apply them. Nancy met Alan in 2005 having ended her career as a college professor, and 18 months later, she was a million dollar consultant using Alan's "game changing," proven techniques and implementing them. This is a 15-year relationship and our second book together.

Innovation is "applied creativity." That is, it is not simply "ideating" but producing ideas that are honed and galvanized into actions that improve the client's (and your) condition. Hence, Nancy's application of Alan's ideas to her own situation—we have very different, successful businesses. Hence, the power of the "speed dating" technique to quickly learn on the need for improvement of ideas so that they can be *applied*.

Once you have validated your ideas, you have a roadmap and a plan for others. You don't need to keep reinventing the wheel, you merely need to keep turning and redirecting it based on the needs and conditions of others.

Here is how you can ask your clients to contribute:

- If you knew you couldn't fail, what would you undertake in the immediate future, personally and professionally?
- What is the highest and best use of your talents and strengths?
- What have you most wanted to do but haven't because you have perceived major obstacles?
- What is the worst that can happen if you tried to implement something important to you, and could you deal with it?
- What is the best that could happen that you may be missing the benefits of right now?
- Are there windows of opportunity closing for you?

These questions can help you with your client to identify whether or not there is enough focus on true innovation, especially nonconformist innovation.

If you ask all your clients every 60 to 90 days questions like this, you will develop patterns and best practices. (In general, if you find something "one-off," it is just an accident; twice, and it is a coincidence; but three times or more and it is probably a pattern.)

Now for the truly counterintuitive: The best ideas *do not* result from "brainstorming sessions" or executive retreats. (I had one client who had so many off-site retreats; I told them they retreated more than Napoleon from Moscow.) Think about the best ideas you have had, and they come from two sources, at least in our experience:

- Privately, while you are focusing on something, in the shower, or watching TV. Suddenly, something hits you. You need to *write it down or record it immediately.* Ergo, we have pads all over to make quick notes. I find them far quicker than electronic means, and they are more readily visible. If the idea makes sense the next day, pursue it. If you can't remember why you wrote it down, then toss it out.

- Coaching others. I get my best ideas coaching others and realizing what I have just advised can be applied in many situations with diverse clients. I make notes of this, as well (if the client is watching, the assumption is you are making notes about the ongoing discussion). Again, I apply the "next day meaning" test, as mentioned earlier. I'm constantly telling people that I learn more than anyone even when I'm coaching or mentoring or responding to questions during a presentation.

Once you have captured a good idea, consider a journal to track what you do with it so that it doesn't "stall" or fall victim to daily vicissitudes. If you can convince your clients to do this, you can jointly review the journal, which I would characterize as "concierge consulting," above and beyond the norm.

As a rule, try to take at least initial actions on innovative ideas within the week, even if it's only the groundwork, in order to put things in motion. "Inertia" is the tendency of an object at rest to stay at rest, and an object in motion to stay in motion. With new ideas we have to "reverse" the inertia, and keep them in motion.

Always focus on *what* you want to accomplish, because once you start examining the "how" to do it too early, someone will assuredly tell you why it can't be done! It was impossible to fly a heavier-than-air craft, impossible to get to the bottom of the Marianas Trench, impossible to conquer Singapore early in World War II, impossible for a Black man (and, at one time, a Catholic) to be President. The "impossible" sometimes just takes a bit longer.

Finally, whether in person or virtually, look for quick, small victories. If you can show early success people will jump on the bandwagon and *find* ways to make it work in as many areas as possible. Take blame for the setbacks but share credit for the advances. The key to innovation, especially with remote people, is that they all feel included in the improvements.

Sources of Innovation

If innovation is not simply creativity and is not created through retreats or workshops, then how is it accomplished? Here are 10 sources of innovation that you can use with your advisory clients to help them examine their own organizations (and lives) to create innovative initiatives and market leadership

Unexpected Success

You might say that success is usually "expected," but we are talking about a past performance that truly exceeded expectations. McDonald's was founded by Ray Kroc, who sold milkshake machines, and received an order for five, each of which was capable of making five milkshakes at a time. He wondered what kind of business generated that volume, found a single burger joint called McDonald's, and realized he was in the same business. An accountant in Rhode Island named Nick Janickes couldn't believe the profits he was seeing in one of his accounts, Burger King, and decided he was better off buying a franchise. He went on to become the largest Burger King franchise owner in New England. The unexpected success of the smart phone has created apps, ear buds, carry cases, and so forth.

Unexpected Failure

Most failures are "unexpected" that one would hope, but they occur regularly. Instead of shunning them or steering clear, we need to ask what the opportunities may be.

The dismal, historic failure of the postal service to deliver anything reliably the next day was a failure that Fred Smith seized on to create FedEx and the hub-and-spoke method of overnight delivery (absolutely guaranteed to get there the next day he unabashedly promised). He didn't try to deliver mail "better," and he began delivering it in a different manner altogether.

Unexpected Event

Remember the power outage at the Dunkin' Donut's store in the Case Study Vignette earlier? That was an unexpected event that had opportunity for the canteen truck owner.

In business, we see sudden departures, new technology, startling competitive actions, consumer desires changing, economic turmoil, and so forth. No one expected the pandemic. But if you had purchased stock in Zoom, you would certainly be smiling a year later.

We have to ask with the unexpected: What is in it for me?

Dramatic Growth

Some of these areas overlap but still deserve separate attention. While smart phones were an unexpected success (they are used primarily not as phones, but as text vehicles, stock trackers, fitness monitors, schedulers, and so forth), they are also examples of stunningly high growth. Whenever such growth occurs, there are opportunities surrounding it, and we can't afford to assume that they don't involve us.

The growth in "clean" energy has created business for solar, wind, and tidal energy; for firms specializing in energy-efficient home adjustments; for utilities offering energy saving consulting advice; for people who can reduce their taxes through clean energy investments and the accountants who can manage that process.

Process Weakness

During the pandemic, take-out food became very popular, but many restaurants were not prepared to provide it rapidly or well prepared. Service arose that picked up from a variety of different restaurants for a fee, enlarging the choice for consumers and eliminating the need for every restaurant to create its own delivery service.

Moreover, containers and packaging were designed to keep food tasty and hot. Credit cards were accepted that included gratuities. The driver simply came to the door and delivered the food piping hot from a special, insulated carrying case. These services will endure no matter what.

Market/Industry Structure Change

Tele-health has upended the health business. Once simply an inventive thought, it is now in wide use for consumers and medical professionals.

(A local hospital here routinely uses closed-circuit TV to include surgeons from a large Boston Hospital to oversee hearth surgery in real time.)

We don't use portals to check on our test results, and we monitor our medications and required medical checkups on our computers. As noted earlier, a smart phone can give us feedback on our current heart rate, pulse, and other factors and remind us of medication schedules.

At one time, hospitals were considered successful if a maximum number of beds were occupied at any one time. Today they are successful in moving people in and out rapidly without lengthy stays. After my wife's hip replacement surgery, she was walking that afternoon and discharged the following day.

Converging Technologies

Welcome to GPS. Converging technologies in automobiles allow for real-time navigation for people, and Uber as an industry. Tele-health uses such combinations. I don't know about you, but I use my iPhone infrequently as a phone, but mostly for e-mail, stock tracking, directions, weather, boarding passes, and so forth.

Demographic Change

This involves change in people's living conditions, income, education, age, and so forth. The largest sector of wealth right now is that of people 65 and above, and they have tremendous buying power. But they don't need a new home, or car, or to save for college education. Right now, the president of TD Bank in the United States told me that they need advisor at all ages for investments, because people want to deal with contemporaries for investment advice.

Perception Change

Perception is reality. The advertising industry is geared to perception change and almost all of your clients are sensitive to it. Our perceptions about climate, immigration, the death penalty, animal abuse, and education have all shifted dramatically, one way or another, within the last decade or so. What are the perceptions of the client organization, and what are the internal perceptions of your client? How can innovation be utilized to advantage? During the pandemic, American Express stopped talking about "Don't leave home without it" because no one was leaving home. Their new campaign: "Don't live life without it." (And Amex, over time, went from green cards to gold, to platinum, and to black emphasizing the perception of a better and more affluent client—prestige.)

New Knowledge

Finally, one might think that new knowledge would be responsible for most innovation, but it is not. In areas such as pharmaceutical research, it is vital, finding new enzyme blockers or cancer cures. But usually organizations don't create innovation through the development of new knowledge, *but rather in using the prior nine categories to better exploit what is already around them.*

We hope you can see the great potential in innovation mastery for yourself and your clients and to use it as a differentiator in your advisory work.

Chapter Return on Investment

- There are three kinds of innovation, all useful.
- Innovation is usually incremental, not the result of retreats or special study.
- Innovation usually comes from the "front lines" where employees deal with customers.
- There are 10 primary sources of innovation.
- Innovation requires prudent risk.
- Don't allow people to "default" to problem solving.
- Your clients and you personally best market through continued improvement of products and service.

CHAPTER 6

Proactive Health Mastery

Have you ever seen a U-Haul in a funeral procession? Your health must be your number first priority, which means you must gain access to leading-edge health resources and technology.

Priority Number One

Your health has to be your first priority and that of your clients. You have to lead by example, even remotely. I shudder every time I watch a professional speaker on stage who is grossly overweight, or a chain smoker, or obviously not very fit, talk to the audience about "taking control of one's life" or "being an exemplar." You can't make this up.

Disease, accident, and illness are often unavoidable, but what matters is what we do about it. Further, what is vital is *prevention* not treatment. You may be thankful for an excellent hospital with superb surgeons, but if what put you there is the fact that you were drinking and driving, you have your priorities mixed up, potentially fatally.

There are companies that have created expensive, comprehensive gyms with trainers to help employees burn off stress after work or at lunch— while piling on the stress during the workday and often in the evenings and weekends. Stress is regarded as the number one cause of illness, and illness is the number one cause of absenteeism at work, and absenteeism at work is the number one employee expense beyond payroll and benefits.

Some people are "proud" of the stress they can handle. Yet stress (like guilt or fear) "masks" talent and never allow one to perform at true potential. That is something to bear in mind as we brag about the stress we can bear.

A dead executive or business owner doesn't make quota! An ill one probably won't either.

For that matter, neither will employees. You will find that your clients advertently or inadvertently place stress on their employees that creates

---

Case Study Vignette

Phil was a coaching client, an entrepreneur in his early 50s with a wife and two children. He had built his business to $650,000 but had four employees who implemented. He was the sole "rainmaker" and spend about 70 percent of his time on the road visiting prospects and clients. He was overweight and a chain smoker.

I was working with Phil to change his business model to advisory work, get rid of most of the employees, and improve his health and lifestyle. He was intellectually on board, but emotionally couldn't make the move (logic makes us think, but emotion urges us to act).

I hadn't heard from him for two weeks, which was unusual, and he missed a scheduled call. I encountered his voice mail when I followed up. Finally, his wife wrote me to say that Phil had died of a heart attack, alone in a hotel room in Boston.

---

sickness and "failure work" and makes your client's job (and life) tougher, not easier.

In Figure 6.1, you can see that at low stress there is usually low productivity. This is a "my right" or "entitlement" mentality, people who believe that the organization is lucky that they are present and that they can take anything that isn't nailed down. There is virtually no accountability for performance. At the extreme right, we see people with huge stress but also low productivity, because they are paralyzed by fear and afraid to move. This is often the case in businesses with frequent layoffs.

In the center is "my pride" that means there is sufficient stress to urge people to meet deadlines, meet or exceed expectations, and give more than expected. The idea isn't to eliminate stress (which is impossible) but rather to manage it correctly. "Eustress" is the opposite of "distress"—it is the stress that is beneficial to the performer. (We bet you probably didn't know that!)

Ask your client where he or she is on this bell curve. Ask for evidence. (Example: Do you enjoy working against a deadline?) Then ask where their employees are, and what evidence they have for their rating. (Example: Are your people comfortable taking prudent risks and innovating?)

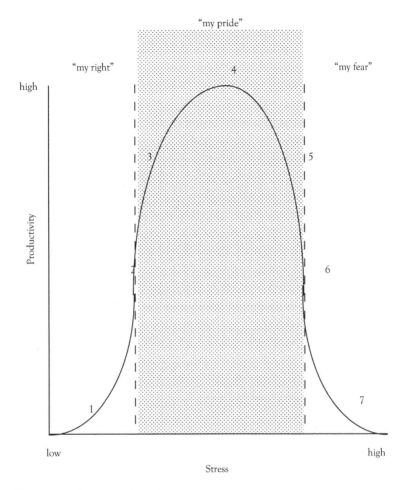

Figure 6.1 Stress and productivity

First, of course, make sure you're solidly planted in the middle your-self, at the peak of the diagram. This is what will enable you to both help your clients rapidly and well *and* help multiple clients at once.

In "sick" organizations or with "sick" people (we will talk about related illnesses later in the chapter) you will find people two or more standard deviations to the left and right. In the former case, stealing from the com-pany and ignoring quality and customers. In the latter case, hiding under their desks and not reporting problems.

If you don't believe that, ask how the scandals at Volkswagen, Enron, Wells-Fargo, and Theranos could possibly have happened if everyone were comfortable and performing excellently and without fear. In our society, people will gladly sign the cast on the broken leg of a friend, but they tend to run and hide if the debility is mental as opposed to physical. There is a great chasm between the acceptance and sympathy for physical problems and that of attempting to deal with mental issues.

I once served on a suicide hotline while pursuing my PhD in psychology. Over 90 percent of the people I talked with over a 20-hour weekly assignment were not at risk for suicide. They were mainly lonely, depressed, addicted, and otherwise having a hard time dealing with hard lives.

But it is not only hard lives that encounter mental problems.

I'm not a clinician not a therapist of any kind. I'm a business coach. But I have been trained to recognize the markers of depression, and this is a key to assisting people (and yourself and your family—depression is hereditary) in mental health. You can't "coach" someone out of depression and any coaching you continue with will be worthless.

Here are markers of depression according to the American Psychiatric Association:

- Feeling sad or having a depressed mood
- Loss of interest or pleasure in activities once enjoyed
- Changes in appetite—weight loss or gain unrelated to dieting
- Trouble sleeping or sleeping too much
- Loss of energy or increased fatigue
- Increase in purposeless physical activity (e.g., inability to sit still, pacing, handwringing) or slowed movements or speech (these actions must be severe enough to be observable by others)
- Feeling worthless or guilty
- Difficulty in thinking, concentrating, or making decisions
- Thoughts of death or suicide

You don't need a PhD or a medical consult. You simply need to be aware of behaviors (exhibiting sadness) or thoughts expressed (worthlessness) that can point you in the right direction.

Case Study Vignette

I was advising the vice president of human resources at a large New York bank. He called me off my current assignment to ask me to handle a special issue.

The bank's executive vice president for investments, Dan, in his early 60s, was an all-star with great performance every year. However, in the current year he seemed to be struggling, his staff was uncertain about direction for the first time during his tenure, and he recently approved a transaction that turned out be a huge error, costing the bank $28 million. The senior team feared Dan was now "too old" and had lost his touch. The vice president with whom I worked wasn't so sure. "Find out what is going on," he told me.

He did not want to meet with me. I finally convinced him to meet with me for breakfast, before work and off-campus, and if he didn't approve of the conversation, we wouldn't meet again. During that breakfast, atop what is not the Met Life Building, he was sullen.

"You seem to lack energy," I observed. "Bad night?"

"I have mostly bad nights," he replied.

"For how long?"

"For about a year or less."

"I understand you are an excellent tennis player, do you still have time for it?"

"Not any more, in fact, I gave my equipment to my son quite a while ago."

As the conversation continued, I realized he was probably clinically depressed. I asked if he were amenable to being tested, and assured him he was dealing with a disease not a loss of talent or abilities.

He agreed, through the company's EAP (employee assistance program) to see a psychologist, was diagnosed with depression, and was provided with both therapy and medication.

Dan's next year at work was his best ever.

Mental health is much more, of course, than being concerned about major abnormalities. It is about keeping yourself positive and involved, composed and productive.

I'm convinced that people wake up in the morning in one of two conditions:

- Another morning, I have bills, some calls I would rather not make, and people who will be rejecting whatever I ask for. It is another long, slow march through enemy territory.
- What a great day, filled with opportunity! I wonder who I will be able to help today!

These attitudes will "color" the rest of the day. How else can you explain, at 7:05 in the morning, a barista who is already rude and sullen, or a newspaper shop employee who is already complaining. And things will get worse from there.

You have seen this in organizations and, perhaps, even with yourself. Here is an exercise you can use and share with your advisory clients:

Every morning, take 60 seconds to think about three positive accomplishments that you will achieve during the day, personally and/or professionally. Every evening, take 60 seconds to review three things you accomplished. These don't have to be major—cleaning out the garage or closing a business deal—but can be steps along the way—cleaning out two shelves in the garage and a prospect agreeing to meet again.

If you would like to read more on this, we suggest *Learned Optimism* that educates you in positive self-talk.[1] The way you talk to yourself informs your behaviors, and your behaviors inform others about your enthusiasm, energy, and abilities. Your clients are often unduly pessimistic because they are where "the buck finally stops." Help them through this to gain mental health.

---

[1] Simon and Schuster (1991).

Emotional Health

Emotional health refers to the ability to manage one's accommodations and reactions to challenge and change. That includes victories and defeats, trauma and celebration, and public and private.

We often hear of emotional intelligence. There is also emotional balance. That is, a proportionate and rational reaction to what occurs to us and around us. Remember, the control point isn't about what happens to us, it is rather what we choose to do about what happens to us.

Emotional distress leaves one susceptible to physical illness, from colds to cancer. What constitutes emotional health, and how can we create and sustain it for ourselves and our clients?

Self-Accommodation

Being in-tune with your body and care for yourself is important. We have talked about physical health and both preventive and contingent measures.

Meaning

Why are we here? How can we serve others? What is our personal calling or mission in life? What is the larger picture that we are part of?

Self-Awareness

This is the opposite of self-absorption and obliviousness. As opposed to the person who stops at the bottom of a crowded, moving escalator to gain his or her bearings, this person knows to quickly step aside and is aware of the surrounding environment and people.

Acceptance

We understand and accept who we are. We don't use other people's metrics to judge our personal success. We don't long to be someone else or to have others' attributes. Judy Garland observed, "I would rather be a perfect me than an imperfect someone else."

Resilience

We need to be agile. We understand that we can't prevent all setbacks or problems. However, we have the agility to overcome and to eventually thrive. We know that "this, too, shall pass."

Humility

We don't mean self-abasement, too commonly associated with humility, but rather the acknowledgment that other people have worth and should be treated kindly and with respect. This is done without demands of reciprocity. We have compassion and tolerance and forgiveness.

Coping

We have the tools needed to deal with situation expected and unexpected. We build up reserves of emotional strength to be used when we are faced with challenge or loss or trauma. These eight traits help us to deal with the inevitable stress and return ourselves constantly to the top of the bell curve in Figure 6.1. We need to practice and sustain our emotional health traits at all times.

Here is an example of resilience:

Figure 6.2 shows the sources of resilience and how they can be applied preventively and contingently. On the left are what we call "hyper-traits" which you can build to create the strengths required to build resilience and emotional health. These traits heighten trust in your own judgment

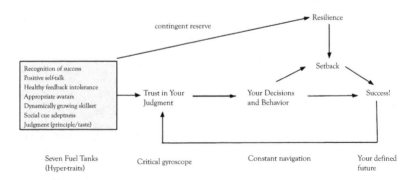

Figure 6.2 Resilience

and improve the critical thinking skills that will be manifest in your behavior (and reaction to unexpected events). The resultant better decisions result in success.

But when they don't, and you encounter setback, that resilience helps you to get back on track. Each success reinforces your confidence in your judgment and further develops those "hyper-traits." So the profession is from your "fuel" to a gyroscope that maintains your bearings (self-awareness, purpose, self-care, and so forth) to an effective navigation to your future.

We find it important—in fact, critical—to be able to explain emotional health in tangible terms, and you should be able to do this with your advisory clients to that you are always discussing pragmatics approaches and not merely philosophy!

That was revelatory from a physical trainer, but absolutely, I'm sure, totally accurate. Our attitudes inform our behaviors, and our behaviors are what others see and have to deal with. Our emotional health plays a huge role in that dynamic.

Ask your clients (and yourself) how you measure up in the aforementioned eight areas and whether you have the "hyper-traits" to retain equanimity and balance no matter what you're facing.

Case Study Vignette

I was observing my personal trainer, Matt, having to constantly urge the two women in the time frame prior to mine to do better and work harder. It didn't seem to me that he was asking too much of them. But they constantly told him they couldn't do what he was asking.

One day I asked him if they were weak physically.

"Not at all," Matt said, "they can certainly do even more than what I'm asking. But they are convinced that they can't do this well. They have serious esteem issues."

"You can tell that from training them?" I asked, stunned.

"Sure, their behaviors reflect their poor emotional states. I would bet that they are totally reliant on their partners at home and seldom take the lead in any initiative, not because they are unable, but because they feel unworthy."

Intellectual Health

Our intellect is our ability to reason and understand objectively. This includes our critical thinking skills.

All of us have opinions and make judgments. I have always loved the admonition "Don't be so judgmental," which, in itself, is judgmental! (It is like those who are told they're too defensive shouting back, "I am *not* defensive!") As trusted advisors, our critical differentiation has to be that of opinion versus fact. The same applies to every leader you are advising. One of the huge problems of the social media age involved opinion passing as fact, and facts being shrugged off as "merely opinions."

We can create our opinions—"I think the economy is better off when small businesses are less regulated"—but we have to acknowledge the facts—small businesses are the largest net, new job producers in North America because larger companies constantly reduce staff through automation, layoffs, and technology.

We often confuse opinion and fact because:

- We don't bother to verify what we were told.
- We ignore what we see in favor of what we would rather believe ("Are you going to believe me or your lying eyes?")
- We are afraid to confront peer pressure.
- We don't know how to find the real evidence.
- We rely on people with personal agendas who distort facts.
- We are too engaged in our own self-interests.

There are two keys to intellectual health and reliable facts:

- What is the empirical evidence? That is, what indisputable facts do we have to support our position, decision, or discussion? An indisputable fact is one that all reasonable people would see as true: Phone are going unanswered, sales are down in Atlanta, the ballpark in only about half-filled.
- What is the observed behavior? That is, what can we agree that we have seen? This would include the fact that the sales

manager is always late for the weekly sales meeting, customers are not walking into the store and merely looking at the window displays, and managers are yelling at subordinates in meetings.

Empirical evidence and observed behavior overlap. Behavior can include, of course, speech and written communications.

Unfortunately, as individuals and as business people, we tend to conflate opinion and fact. You can see in the aforementioned case how important it is to present facts (as opposed to, "My opinion is that people will leave if you don't change Ricky's behavior).

To have healthy client relationships, you have to be healthy yourself.

Case Study Vignette

I was called in to coach Rick who was the son of the late owner of the firm and an executive vice president. Rick abused people in the hallways. He used profanity, questioned their abilities, threatened their continued employment. He was also heading the most profitable division of the business. He had already been "coached" by three other people, to no avail.

The president, Paul, installed by the new owners, a Fortune 100 company, asked me to work with Rick. Rick told me that he wasn't interested in being coached, and I should leave his office. He was obscene is his comments.

I told Paul that Rick had to be fired. He told me that his opinion was that "Rick was Rick" and his performance overcame some "random complaints." I explained that everyone I spoke to blamed him, the president, on the basis that Rick couldn't act that way without the president's blessing, and that he was actually the president's surrogate.

"You will have a hard time explaining that to the board at the annual meeting," I pointed out. The fact is that you can stop this by removing him, or you can continue to tolerate it and be blamed for it.

Rick was fired the next day.

Chapter Return on Investment

- You need physical, emotional, mental, and intellectual health.
- Preventive "medicine" and procedures are always better than having to find a "cure."
- Create regular physical checkups.
- Use positive self-talk.
- Focus on observed behavior and empirical evidence.
- Separate opinion from fact and identify which is which.
- Validate opinions so that they can become fact.
- Learn to recognize medical issues that might require attention.

CHAPTER 7

Relationship Mastery

A relationship is a "connectedness." The nature of the relationship determines how two people (or groups) behave toward each other, support each other, trust each other. Trusted advisors must, above all, create relationships that no only support others, but inspire them.

The Lifeline

Trusting relationships must honor confidentiality. We have learned, of the hard way, that there are no "secrets" in organizations, large or small. When we were told, "I want to share a secret with you," it is no longer a secret and we should know immediately we are not the only ones who privy to it.

But honoring trust and creating a lifeline for our clients means more than confidentiality. It means tough love.

Telling someone they are performing better than they are isn't an effective device to motivate them. It is a dysfunctional device that stunts their development. Trust is about being honest, and honest often involves pain. We would rather know we have lettuce in our teeth through someone's kindness rather than enter the meeting that way, and we would rather know that our presentation is ineffective in rehearsal rather than delivering it that way.

Relationships aren't compartmentalized, but rather holistic. It is important to be aware of and sensitive to your client's life—family, interests, background, experiences, and so forth. These issues affect how people make decisions, their perspective, and our ability to help. You

Advisory: Tough love is a sign of caring.

shouldn't attempt to be therapeutic—we are not clinicians—but you should feel comfortable understanding your client's circumstances. Working a 60-hour week is one thing if you live alone and another if you have a family.

The principle with a "lifeline" built on trust is that the advisor is the first one called, the person who can immediately make a critical difference. There is the confidence that if you can't help, you will say so, and find someone who can. But more often than not, you can help.

Thus, you are adding value to the lives of your clients with every interaction. You practice "tough love," telling the truth even when it "hurts," knowing the longer-term gain is worth it. You don't make judgments, don't foist opinions on others, but use observed behavior and evidence in the environment to support your help. When you have the courage to provide tough feedback, you give them the courage to provide it to others themselves.

The characteristics of trusted advisor relationship mastery include:

- True caring about the person client beyond their being simple a "client."
- Objective assessment of performance with nonjudgmental feedback.
- Your courage with feedback provides them with the courage to provide tough feedback and confidently make tough decisions.
- You challenge them to grow. You don't mistake a plateau or complacency for growth.
- You maintain absolute confidentiality and honor all commitments and deadlines.
- You allow for vulnerability, sharing mistakes, errors, and regrets.
- You expect to be and are the first person they call in most challenging situations.
- Neither of you withhold reactions or observations.
- You challenge beliefs and assumptions for force objective decisions and rational behaviors.

The "Evergreen" or Lifetime Trusted Advisor Relationship

Coaching is a process of helping someone achieve certain behavioral objectives. These may include presenting at meetings, providing performance evaluations, speaking on state, writing promotional pieces, facilitating meetings, and so forth. Coaching is for a finite period—we would say no more than 90 days—because after that there's a tendency for it to become codependency.

If someone can't do something they want to do—whether write a speech or clean out the garage—there is a strong probability that they are not going to be able to do it at all no matter how much time is allocated. And if they can't get it accomplished in 90 days of less of expert coaching, it is probably not something for them at all. Hire a speechwriter and get a handyman.

However, a trusted advisor forms a relationship that is a sounding board, access to the advisor's "smarts." Usually, the stronger someone is, and the more confident, the more comfortable they are using advisors. Presidents, CEOs, star athletes, great entertainers, foundation chairs—they all use advisors (and many may use coaches periodically, as well).

Case Study Vignette

Mastering relationships with your trusted advisor peers is game changing. Most trusted advisors are lone wolves and it doesn't serve them well to be in this role. During Covid, Nancy launched 90-day peer groups for trusted advisor Forum Chairs so they could build lifeline relationships with each other. This helped them raise their game on mastering relationships with their clients because they learned from each other's successes and failures.

Of course, most of the trusted advisor Forum Chairs are having their best year ever in 2020 because they made the decision to learn from their peers how to establish even deeper relationships with their clients. And, the 90-day peer groups will live on forever because once you find a best fit peer group, you want to be on the journey of life with them forever.

The trusted advisor relationships create "evergreen" clients because the more you work with someone, the more they trust you. The more they trust you, the more they seek to use you. After all, you are not vested in the company's retirement program, you are not after a corner office, and you don't want your client's job.

You are simply there to help as a source of expertise and a sounding board.

We have found that evergreen advisory relationships require these traits and focus:

- Generosity: You have to there for your client professionally and personally. Stop short of the boundaries of your expertise (e.g., therapy, health), but be willing to talk about and help with the client's relationships, interests, fears, regrets, and so forth. Demonstrate empathy (not sympathy) in understanding and relating to another's feelings.
- Reciprocity: Demonstrate that you are peers by disclosing your own fears and expectations, and eliciting the client's opinions. If your child is having trouble deciding on a college, ask what process your client used.

Case Study Vignette

The CEO of Calgon, Forrest, had me serve as a trusted advisor for five years—until he retired and the company was sold. Once a month he had a Tuesday morning board meeting.

Forrest would call me on Monday nights to review his plans and presentation and get my feedback—during halftime of Monday Night Football. He didn't like football, but he knew that I did, so he made it a habit to call and conclude our conversation during halftime.

Starting our third of five years, I send my usual bill for $100,000 on January 2 to cover the ensuing year. But he told me he wasn't paying it. He said that I was more important than that and he was paying me $130,000.

I didn't object.

- Innovation: Never be satisfied merely solving problems. Strive to innovate. For example, we have launched "speed dating" in which we attempt to identify valuable new business opportunities within an eight-minute time frame. Just as meetings where you are forced to stand tend to end earlier, the time limit tends to force ideas to the surface without self-editing.

- Attraction: I use an approach called "the chain reaction of attraction"®. This brings great value to any one client through introductions to others whom they otherwise would never have met. There is huge intrinsic value and relationship building in providing these interactions. The more you attract others, who are themselves attractors, the greater the chain reaction you create.

- Inclusion: Whether a closely-held firm or a Fortune 1000 giant, consider your client's family in your discussions. It is helpful to learn their names and what occupies them. "Life balance," after all, is about leading seamless life, not a compartmentalized one.

- Accountability: Periodic reviews to ascertain whether commitments are fulfilled and deadlines met are key to relationship success. We aren't involved to simply commiserate, but rather to hold each other accountable for our goals.

Guidelines for Holistic Relationship Mastery

Advisory work isn't "evergreen" unless you work to make it so. A pine or a fir tree is preprogrammed in the tree's "DNA." But people need to grow and work to become tall and strong.

Advisor can be fired at any time. President Trump seemed to fire advisors daily. Athletes fire managers, teams fire coaches. You have to maintain

> *Advisory: Relationship mastery is a process, not a "deliverable," and can by repeated with every client.*

Case Study Vignette

My CEO advisory client and I and our wives had dinner together in the very staid, very impressive Duquesne Club in Pittsburgh. We were washing up and I was astonished (he was the member) in the grand, ornate, huge men's room.

"Why don't we show our wives?" I suggested.

"You know, my wife has never seen this, and originally a men's club, I'm sure this outdoes the Ladies Room!"

We made sure it was empty, we stood guard at the door, and our wives had a good laugh together. That' is what relationships can provide.

Advisory: Too many advisors are actually deciduous, and lose their leaves (and their clients)!

---

a winning record and demonstrate to the client that his or her life and business are better because of you.

In fact, in some cases you may create the perception that they can't thrive without you.

Often, advisors simple raise their fees without providing any additional value. Certainly the cost of the call hasn't risen precipitously, and you should never use existing clients to subsidize new clients. Here are some guidelines for remaining evergreen:

- Solicit feedback from your buyer. What has worked well and what has not worked so well? Is the method and frequency of feedback correct or too infrequent (or too frequent)? Never assume that your perception is shared by the buyer. Find out your true value.
- Never place blame on your client. If something isn't working, don't cite a missed deadline or error as if you are a tutor teaching business hygiene. Share the responsibility. (And give your client all the credit.) Say, "WE didn't adequately prepare for…" instead of, "Why didn't you follow my advice and prepare for…"

Case Study Vignette

Some years ago, a survey was conducted about how the clients of New York City advertising firms felt about their service. Stunningly, the clients felt better about the services provided *than the ad companies felt about it.*

Think about that. The repercussions, because of that misperception, of lower fees than should have been charged, more servicing and attention than may have been required, more resources assigned than might have been necessary.

The analogy is quite apt. You need to understand how your client perceives and values the relationship. This will not only influence your actions and behaviors with them, but also with future clients.

Defensiveness: Some advisors are outraged when the client also takes advice from others! Sometimes it's formalized, as with a coach or another firm. Sometimes its informal, as in family members or business peers (remember the power of peer-level reference).

Advisors get into a huff and may even chastise the client about listening to someone else or some other source. ("What, you actually listened to a Harvard Professor!?) What you need to do is listen first, then assimilate, then try to support what will work and frustrate what might not *always focused on your client's best interests.*

Taking umbrage or leaving in a huff when told of alternative input is a great way to lose a client and referrals permanently and turn the leaves from green to brown. (I have always thought about buying stock in "umbrage" and "huff" since they are so frequently patronized!)

Holistic mastery includes the consideration of these factors, as well:

- Serve on boards with your client, especially nonprofits and community causes. Or contribute to those causes your client (and/or your client's spouse and/or family) supports. If your client is seeking a pet, suggest a good rescue operation to visit for adoption.

- Exchange travel and entertainment and recreation ideas with your client, and give each other feedback. You don't need to take up beach volleyball just because your client likes it, but you may want to visit the island on which the tournament is held.
- Plan a visit and meeting in a nice spot and invite your family. You might take two days out of a two-week vacation to meet with your client, and have a collective dinner one night. (Always try to pick up a dinner check, though in some cases, it is against corporate policy to allow a service provider to pay for anything, so be sensitive to the situation.)
- Expand your own network and client base so that you can provide even better frames of reference and perspective for your clients. Never "coast." Set the example by constantly growing and stretching yourself.

The Constancy of Change and the Need for Support

Lady Gaga was nominated for an Oscar for best actress in a leading role in 2019 (*A Star is Born*) and won the Oscar for best original song (from that show, "Shallow").

She was born Stephanie Germanotta. Her original record label dumped her. She entered the world of cabaret, garnered support, worked like crazy to get in shape, overcame the critiques about not looking good enough and not talented enough, and metamorphosed into Lady Gaga who is a role model and inspiration to millions of people (as well as a great singer).

The legendary audition summary of Fred Astaire noted that he had thinning hair, a weak voice, and "danced a little." There is a great song from the Broadway musical "A Chorus Line" entitled "Dance Ten, Looks Three," which encourage the actress in the role to obtain plastic surgery. But there also a line in the show that states, "I am not my résumé."

Over the past decade, Americans alone have probably spent $300 billion on weight loss measures. That is not a typo.[1] Yet, we are heavier than

---

[1] www.bmc.org/nutrition-and-weight-management/weight-management

> **Case Study Vignette**
>
> It was lonely for trusted advisors pre-Covid, and it is even worse now for trusted advisors who don't have a top 20 list of relationships that they are nurturing. Nancy encouraged trusted advisor Forum Chairs to set up an advisory board (of clients and other trusted advisors) and to always have a top 20 list of relationships each quarter to keep them inspired and to help them master relationships. This has been game changing for our trusted advisor forum chairs.

ever! The average weight for an adult woman is about 165 pounds, and for a man 195 pounds.

Spending money isn't the issue. Finding help isn't the issue. Most people can spend money and find help.

Accountability and discipline are the issues. In most cases, people can lose weight with little expenditure through exercise and changed eating habits. In most cases, people can learn to dress well and apply makeup correctly, to improve their singing voice (or any other talent), and to overcome mistaken and unfair evaluations and critique.

Imagine if Lady Gage or Fred Astaire had a career terminated early by poor reviews or an occasional poor performance. Our job in relationship mastery, as trusted advisors, is to help our client to understand:

1. They can change and improve if they're committed to doing so.
2. That change and improvement are ongoing because conditions change. At this writing, Tony Bennet is still singing in his 90s, as he has been for 70 years. And guess who he sometimes appears with and records with: Lady Gaga.
3. That we can be a trusted support and resource for those changes and improvement in our advisory roles.

Your relationship mastery will enable you to form communities of people whom rely on you and rely on each other. *The ability to connect people who otherwise would not have known each other, let alone grown and prospered from knowing each other, is huge.* Alan has even created a trademarked

> *Advisory: The stronger your support system, the better your accountability and discipline are likely to be.*

phrase for this: The chain reaction of attraction®. This means that as you attract people who are attractive to others, and who begin to help each other, your community and your relationships grow exponentially.

Hence, we use the term "relationship mastery" because you need the skills and discipline to manage your community. Those who had these relationships and communities in place prepandemic in 2020 *had far more success and business growth than others.* That is because an interconnectedness and reliance was already in place, it did not have to be created.

People who maintained these communities:

- Had a vehicle to share best practices
- Were not reliant on physical events and the danger of their cancellation, since virtual communications were already in place
- Could offer immediate, substantive help to their members
- Developed national and global perspectives on business conditions and opportunities
- Solidified the reliance on the community and, therefore, the community leader

When you organize groups of people who interact to help each other, and who didn't know each other before your creation of the relationships, all of that value accrues to you, enabling you to further expand your ability to help others.

This is what the modern trusted advisor role is all about.

Chapter Return on Investment

- Our clients need "lifelines" that we can provide.
- Honesty, generosity, and candor are hallmarks of the trusted advisor.

- "Evergreen" clients result from effective, trusting relationships.
- Accountability of both parties is critical.
- "Public" accountability is always more effective.
- The relationship is about the person not just the business.
- To be truly effective, you must take a "holistic" approach.
- Communities are valuable and essential for people to grow.
- Change is a needed constant. The point is to manage it and not be managed by it.

CHAPTER 8

Passion Mastery

Use your passion, strengths, purpose, "your why" to make the biggest impact every single day.

The Extraordinary

Our formula for passion mastery is that passion + competence + need = extraordinary results. We need all three.

Think about the lack of any one:

Competency and passion but no market need: No one hears your message.

Competency and market need but no passion: A 9 to 5 job.

Passion and market need but no competency: You lose to the competition.

As we have mentioned, emotion urges people to act and creates a sense of immediacy. Your passion is contagious. Not nearly enough people are bold or passionate enough to say, "I can help you," "We can start immediately," or even, "Let me put a proposal in front of you."

The first question I ask my advisory clients is: "Are you having fun?" The reaction is consistently one of surprise, as if a leader isn't supposed to have fun. Yet engaging in one's passion is fulfilling. Hobbies and interests invoke passion, why shouldn't one's "calling"?

We need to dedicate some time to the consideration of our passion. Simply focusing on the other two factors—competency and need—create a "grind" if there is no fulfillment.

We improve by building on strengths, not correcting weaknesses. What are your true strengths? To what extent are you employing them daily?

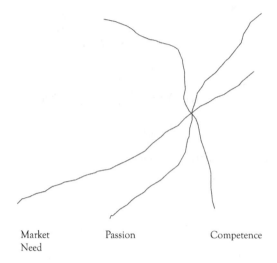

Market   Passion   Competence
Need

Figure 8.1 Extraordinary formula

Case Study Vignette

When I was fired, there were more than 250,000 independent consultants in the United States alone, many (most/) of whom had a huge head start over me, and who had clients and track records as independents.

I didn't ask what they were doing and how I could emulate it. I asked, instead, "What am I really good at?" The answer was writing and speaking. I hated networking and didn't believe in advertising.

So, I wrote and spoke, wrote and spoke. Today, I have more than 60 commercially published books in 15 languages, I'm in the Speakers Hall of Fame® and I have the strongest solo consulting brand in the world. I doubt any of that would have happened if I tried to copy others and "fix" what I didn't do as well as they did.

Solicited feedback is a great way to validate your strengths. Here is the formula for how best to do this:

- List what you believe are your outstanding strengths.
- Ask a friend or colleague (or small group of them) what they think your outstanding strengths are.

- Compare the lists. Reconcile the differences, for example, "I have never seen you do that," "I only see you at work," or "I don't think you realize you're doing this." Don't forget to look at empirical evidence and observed behavior.
- Once reconciled, determine how much of the time you actually employ your greatest strengths. In all activities? Daily? Only when you remember to use them?
- Devise a plan, with others' help, on how to more often "default" to these strengths. (e.g., If you make points excellently telling stories, what will prompt you to use stories more often?)

We all have "blind spots" that prohibit us from learning more about ourselves and, when we actually do, we tend to focus on weaknesses, as though we need to be "fixed" in some manner. Your advisory clients are the same.

Think about how useful this preceding simple exercise would be with your clients.

You may recognize that there are similarities with the very popular 360° feedback approaches. However, unlike those approaches we're focusing strictly on strengths, and asking people we respect who know us, not necessarily subordinates or peers. And we are involving the personal as well as professional side. Strengths are strengths no matter what the environment.

It's important to consider *patterns* and not one-off feedback. An individual may be accurate in reporting something no one else sees or experiences, but if that behavior or strength is not common enough for others to also report it you should not make it a priority. (The same applies to weaknesses, by the way. One person who doesn't like your approach may say more about them than you. "I have never read a single one of your books," someone once told me haughtily. "How unfortunate for you," I said, and walked away.)

This is especially important because your typical advisory client *does not* receive objective, unfiltered feedback on the average day—or, perhaps, *ever*. Subordinates don't feel bold enough and if they do feel they are commenting positively on a strength it can be seen as sycophantic. Peers seldom bother to point out strengths, often because of an implicit or explicit rivalry or competition. Superiors often feel that it's their job to find fault, not to praise.

And as for family, here is a saying I keep on my desk that I can read daily:

> *A prophet is not without honor except in his native place and among his own kin and in his own homer.*
>
> —The Gospel of Mark 6:4

Passion mastery can lead to extraordinary results if all the components are present and reinforced on a continuing basis. And that is an ideal role for a trusted advisor.

The Purpose Behind Passion

We often lead onerous lives. We have problems with our families, in our community, in our careers. We're faced with challenges that demand we take actions we are not motivated to begin. These feelings are not "compartmentalized." They "bleed-over" and one area affects all other areas of our lives.

I have always viewed what I do as a "sport." It is a healthy competition. I enjoy meeting new prospects, love being in their offices in reality or virtually. I enjoy applying the tough love that is often required to force someone to come to terms with issues that are causing a roadblock.

My advice for people who want referral business, for example, is to call only three people a day. Surely that is a manageable number. And they should have their comments and request prepared, always asking for referrals by name—not, "can I have some names" but rather "can you introduce me to your counterpart on the West Coast."

If you ever face an advisor call or relationship as something onerous, you are in the wrong business. You are just laying bricks, and you are not bringing people closer to God! The purpose behind passion is that it's never burdensome because the mere pursuit fulfills you.

I have watched people who have interests and hobbies which they treat like "work." They say things like, "I have to go work on my hobby."

That is quite an oxymoron! A hobby is supposed to offer relief and no stress, not add to the work day or compete for time!

Passion is "unbridled emotion." It is an intense feeling of satisfaction and fulfillment. Ideally, you should be passionate about your work. Remember, even with a market need and great skills, without passion you have merely a job.

Ask yourself, and your advisory clients:

- What is my purpose? Is it fulfilling?
- Do I have a mission?
- How do I know I'm successful in that mission and calling?
- Is my default position happiness and enthusiasm?

You can teach someone the content of any business, be it automotive brake pads or insurance contracts. But you can't "teach" anyone enthusiasm, or energy, or extroversion. Those are behaviors that are innate, but they can be coached and improved if not sufficiently present.

We tend to "dampen" these native behaviors because we are afraid of offending people, or being seen as "taking over" or not giving others a "chance." But our calling is about inspiring and improving others—in return for equitable compensation—and therefore we have to engage people in a positive and compelling manner. This is easiest and best done when we are eager to do so, not fearful, and when we are "other-oriented" and not self-absorbed.

Humility is about recognizing the worth of others, not debasing ourselves. I have never heard anyone demand that someone find a humbler heart surgeon, or litigator, or, for that matter, advisor. People need talent and candor to achieve the improvements they need.

The lawyer had a very narrow focus, equating his work with his "passion." But he was simply a workaholic. We all have met these people. They can't chat about world events, or sports, or the latest movies. They don't know about good restaurants, or cars, or vacation spots.

They are boring.

Extrapolate those weaknesses to their careers and you find professionals who are dull outside of their specialty. These people are always suspect to me. Being well-rounded is part of being attractive to others. I don't like

---

Case Study Vignette

I was a guest lecturer at Boston College talking to an evening class of professionals who were seeking higher degrees. The subject was life balance.

"My balance is merely doing my work," said Harry, a partner in a law firm. "I love my work and have no qualms about working until 2 am six days a week and sometimes seven. I typically work about 60 hours in the office weekly."

"Does your son play sports?" I asked.

"Yes, he plays soccer."

"Did you teach him anything about the sport?"

"No, he has had coaches for that."

"How many of his games have you seen?"

"I try to see one or two a season, but it is not always possible. But don't ask me how I feel about that, because my work enables him to be able to be coached and play soccer."

"I would be more concerned about how he feels about it, because he is never going to be seven again although your job will always be there."

---

financial advisors who can only talk about money, or legal advisors who can only talk about legal precedents. I want tax experts who understand my family and life objectives.

I sat next to the second ranking officer in the Providence police force, whom I know, not long ago by accident, having dinner at a bar. We talked of several things, but I had to specifically ask him about police work before he began talking about it. He is clearly in his position and an excellent leader because he is so well-rounded. I think that makes him especially effective in his community.

There are people arising every morning who simply don't know what their purpose is! They don't think about it. The go through the motions and "grind" out their day. You can't afford to do that and you can't afford to allow your clients to do that. *Carpe Diem*. You have to seize the day.

| Apathy | Awareness | Interest | Emotionalism | Zealotry |

And that's best done when you are passionate about what you can do that way.

The Limits of Passion

People can be passionate about their work, religion, the stock market, relationships, or the Los Angeles Dodgers. There is a continuum of passion that might look like this:

It has been said that "There is no zealot like the converted." This is usually based on St. Paul, a virulent tormentor of Christians until his epiphany on the road to Damascus, where he became the greatest chronicler of Jesus and Christianity in history. (Without the prolific writings of Paul, we would know very little about those times.)[1]

In other words, like any emotion, passion need to be controlled and productively applies. Fans at ballgames ("fan" comes from "fanatic") can support and help their teams—the famous "home field advantage." But fans can also become boisterous, rowdy, and result in the kind of soccer game mayhem we often see reported in Europe that result in injury and even death. There have been fights, assaults, and even murder reported among parents at kids' athletic games. Infamously, one father was arrested for sharpening the hardware on his son's football helmet so that it would be painful to tackle him.

I remember being in a hotel once where there was a Jell-o convention (this was the famous flavored gelatin). In the mornings, the staff would get together and sing the Jell-o fight song! In many Japanese plants, it is not unusual for employees to sing a motivational song at the start of a shift. "We are number one" is not just something we here at sports events. And even at the Olympics, where it is how you play the game not whether

---

[1] In reality, people who switch religions today show a modestly more degree of passion to the new faith. (Pew Research Center: www.pewforum.org/2009/10/28/the-zeal-of-the-convert-is-it-the-real-deal/).

you win, they keep track of medal counts and play the winner's national anthem after every event.

One of the keys about passion is where we direct it. As you can see in In Figure 8.2, 100 percent of our talent and energy are directed either internally—within the organization—or externally, toward the client, product, service, and relationship. (When people say, "Give me 110 percent!" I have no idea what that means.)

Thus, our passion has to be directed to growing the business, delighting the customer, gaining referrals, and so forth. *It can't be directly to getting the corner office, taking credit for success, maximizing one's bonus.* That is because of the 100 percent factor: Every ounce of passion, and the commensurate talent and energy, that goes into office politics or gossip or unimportant matters, is an ounce that won't go toward the customer—the lifeblood of the business.

What should those percentages be? How do you test this with your advisory clients (and, of course, with your own practice)?

My experience is 20 percent internal and 80 percent external. (Interestingly, this doesn't change with remote work as ideals, but the actuality, of course, does.) If 80 percent of your passion goes toward the customer and prospect, you will have a thriving business, assuming you have good people. However, in this "hydraulic system," is those percentages shift

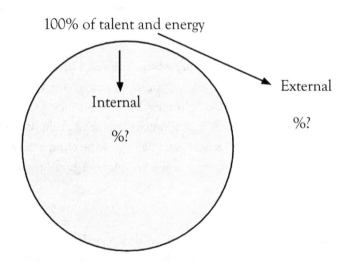

Figure 8.2 The application of passion

to internal, you will have an inefficient and struggling business which consumes the time of leaders and undermines their strategy.

When a company must reduce staff, it should do so in one complete, bold move. When you "string out" layoffs, no one works, everyone begins to "hide," and focus is 99 percent internal and one percent external. Customers begin to disappear. (Picture a solo practitioner focused on excessive debt and family problems with no time going toward building the business.) In Figure 6.1 of Chapter 6, you would position such people on the extreme right, paralyzed by fear and totally unproductive.

Hence, the key tactic for your clients is to focus people *externally* on the clients and prospects. You probably can't avoid the 20 percent or so of "grapevine" gossip that will continue, but bear in mind this gets worse with remote workers whom no one is observing regularly. That 20 percent ideal becomes 40 percent or worse if you consider distractions caused by a home environment and family presence.

We want to create passion short of zealotry. *We want to influence and persuade, not "convert."*

Since we know that emotion prompts people to act and creates urgency, we should pursue the "emotional" stage on the aforementioned continuum. And this brings us to a final, vital point here.

Passion is about outcomes. It is about goals and future conditions. I realize that it is important to fix the roof, but that is a required task. However, I can get passionate about finding a new home. I'm not passionate about working out with my trainer (although you will find training zealots, just as you will diet zealots). But I am passionate about along, healthy life and watching my grandchildren grow up. I wasn't passionate about college and too many boring lectures, but I was passionate about what I could to with the ensuing learning.

Of course, many people are passionate about relationships, but not commitment, about a wonderful evening together but not about a shared lifetime. Unfortunately, many are swayed by the temporary activities and then must endure (or end) unhappy results. No one is ecstatic about cleaning up after a new puppy, but people love their pets.

Work with your clients to engage their passion about results they can achieve and the tasks along the way will become much easier to undertake.

Make sure you do that yourself—you may not enjoy asking for referrals, but I would guess that you are passionate about new business.

Remember, no one really *needs* a drill. What they *need* are holes.

Joy

With money in your pocket, you are smart, good looking, and you sing well, too.

Joy is the feeling of great pleasure and happiness. This is why I ask my advisory clients if they are having fun and if they are happy. Working productively and successfully, and being happy and fulfilled, are synergistic, not antithetical. One reinforces the other.

Dan Gilbert is Edgar Pierce Professor of Psychology at Harvard University, and is someone I've had the pleasure of hosting at one of my events. He wrote *Stumbling on Happiness* (Alfred A. Knopf 2016) in which he discusses people's ability to be happy and the ramifications. One of his findings (in my words, not his) is that "synthetic happiness" is as important as conventional happiness.

Convention happiness occurs when you might expect it to: birthdays, anniversaries, graduations, holidays, victories, promotions, and so forth. But we all are also familiar with synthetic happiness:

> Losing that job was the best thing that ever happened to me.
> That hospital stay helped me to reprioritize my life.
> Missing the game actually drew us closer together.

These "rationalizations," according to Gilbert, do produce happiness and joy. To my mind, they are attitudes.

People who are optimistic seem somehow to always make the best of things. I'm not talking about blind optimism, where you simply trust the best will happen or you believe the fates will be kind to you. I'm talking about "rational optimism" where we see the possibilities and opportunities in a situation, experience, or circumstance.

We all have occasion to be sad, depressed, gloomy, and even morose. But those are the exceptions, not the norm, for successful people. I recall a coffee shop owner we used to call "Gloomy Gus." When it rained, he

Case Study Vignette

As I write this, we are emerging from the Covid pandemic. A significant portion of the population has been vaccinated (in the United States and other countries), stimulus money is fueling hiring and investment, the stock market is soaring, and people are beginning to travel and engage in entertainment and recreation outdoors.

Many businesses were prepared for this, with the attitude that things can only get better, there are obvious signs of renewal and it is important to prepare for success.

Other businesses have a "hunker down" mentality of saving every penny and being archly conservative, convinced that it is still a long way to safety and that the worst isn't over.

The former businesses will surf the crest of this new growth wave, and the latter will be tossed about by it. It is not a difference of sector, or service, or clientele. It is a difference in attitude.

said business was bad because people didn't want to get out of their cars. When it was sunny, he said business was bad because people preferred to drive farther away. Times were never good for him, not empirically, but in his opinion.

His attitude carried over to his service. No one wants to visit a coffee shop first thing in the morning and be depressed!

Let us define "meaning," as you see in Figure 8.3, as "significance." In other words, the importance of events or circumstances. The graphic juxtaposes it with happiness.

A successful life (upper left quadrant) is one of high meaning and high happiness. You are contributing, providing value, and receiving value. There is a strong reciprocity. You love and are loved. These are the most productive people I have ever met.

In the upper left, there is high happiness but low meaning. This is an addictive personality, one requiring stimulus but not necessarily quality outcomes. A drug addiction provided temporary happiness without any meaning at all. Workaholics would be in this category, in that there

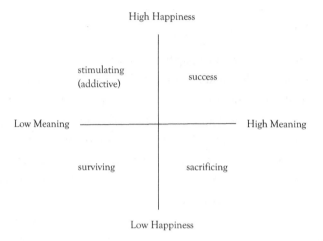

Figure 8.3 Happiness and meaning

is a diminishing return in terms of the nonessential, additional hours invested. These are often the perfectionists or, in my world, the people who insist on point out typos but don't comment on the content.

When the converse occurs (lower right) you are engaged in activities and pursuits of high meaning but they don't make you happy. They are not fulfilling. The humorist George Ade said once, "Don't pity the martyrs, they love the work." These are people who toil in worthwhile jobs and make contributions, but aren't motivated by them and don't feel appreciated.

Finally, people who are merely surviving (lower left) are those going through the motions. Every day of their life is the same as the day before. There is no hope, there is no happiness.

Next we will take a look at our responsibility to achieve the upper right status for ourselves and our clients.

Chapter Return on Investment

- Passion plus competence plus need equals extraordinary results.
- We tend to overlook the importance of passion.
- Understand your strengths and build on them, and don't focus on correcting weaknesses—you are not "damaged."

- Are you allocating your time to what you are passionate about, and are you passionate about what is most important in your work and life?
- Use solicited feedback to determine your strengths.
- Understand your purpose and commit yourself to living it.
- Reflect on what gives you joy and happiness.
- Allow yourself to be happy.
- Adopt an attitude of rational optimism.
- Make sure your energy and talent are directed externally at the customer/client, relationship, product, and/or service.

CHAPTER 9

100 Percent Responsibility Mastery

Believe in yourself and avoid victim consciousness/playing the blame game. Show up as the "real you"—caring, vulnerable, and assertive every day.

The Abundance Mindset

Every day, we have to use a 100 percent responsibility and 0 percent criticism mindset. This is empowering. The opposite is self-defeating. Thoreau's famous observation was "Most men live lives of quiet desperation." Too many men and women today live with a scarcity and poverty mindset.

Let us return to Figure 4.1, the watertight doors.

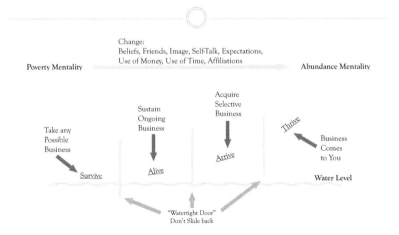

We pointed out that to move from poverty and scarcity toward abundance, we must make *changes* or we would forever have a scarcity mentality no matter how "successful" our lives otherwise were.

We have to learn to treat ourselves and others as the possessors of unique, human gifts, and talents. Specifically:

- You have to be authentic, in the sense that you are honest and candid, and be ready to share your defeats and setbacks as well as your victories and successes.
- You exhibit vulnerability, in that you are nondefensive and open to solicited feedback, considering the views of others for the possible improvement of your own behavior and results.
- You are "judgment-free" in that you seek causes and not blame. When you do find individual error or failings, you attempt to help and improve the poor performance, not condemn it.

Case Study Vignette

I was working with Ron, the CEO of a specialty eyewear company. He was very bright and energetic, and his company was doing well. However, he felt his team wasn't sufficiently responsive and engaged.

I shadowed him for two weeks in meetings, presentations, evaluations, and so forth. At our debrief, I noted his observed behavior that concerned me the most: "Ron, you constantly cut people off. You finish their sentences and then move on to the next subject. Do you recall the executive meeting just yesterday when you did that to your CFO and your sales director?"

"I do," he said, "but my motivation is to move things along and show them that I'm with them and agree."

"How long are you conscious that you have been doing this?"

"That's how I got on the 'fast track' at the company, by being the smartest guy in the room when I was in a room full of bright people."

"But you are not that guy and you are not in that room anymore. Now you have different responsibilities, to bring out the best in others and not continually demonstrate that you're the best, right?"

Ron changed his manner, stopped thinking that he was competing in a scarcity environment, and his team became far more productive.

- You assume responsibility. "What could I have done better to have earned this business?" (or get this promotion, or succeed in this assignment) is the question, rather than blaming others.
- You don't hold grudges. You don't seek "revenge." When you hold someone else responsible for your troubles, you can never be freed, because that person is usually unaware whether he or she is being "blamed." If you don't "let to," you will be troubled forever by ancient "slights."
- You don't take out your own unhappiness by judging and critiquing others. Most anger is actually self-directed anger that we reorient toward others so as not to damage ourselves emotionally. We have to admit our own errors and move on without anger.
- You must use your own metrics. Our self-esteem should be constant, our self-worth acknowledged. Don't judge your own progress by how fast someone else runs, how rapidly they write, or how well they speak. And don't be intimidated by others who do things well.
- You need to love yourself in order to love others. If you are happy with yourself, you can be happy with others, tolerate their shortcomings, and rejoice in thieve successes.
- Your self-esteem is not based on your latest victory or defeat, we all will win some and lose some. This doesn't affect our worth as people.

You might say, "Whew, that's an overwhelming list, I don't know if I'm up to that!" But you are, we all are. This is about mindset.

We have both facilitated retreats with senior people in diverse organizations and all too frequently we find these issues arising. If you are a veteran advisor, we are sure that you have seen the same thing. If you are new to the profession in this capacity, then prepare yourself for it. It is actually heartbreaking to see people with huge potential and the ability to help others suffer from esteem issues *for which they are not taking personal responsibility.*

This is where you can be of huge help. You must take the responsibility for confronting the behaviors in the points listed earlier. This is what "tough love" is all about, the responsibility of being honest and confronting in order to help your client.

Ron wasn't evil or insecure. He has simply not sufficiently changed to embrace abundance, and hadn't grown comfortable with his own self-worth.

Masking Your Own Talent

There are emotions and conditions that tend to "mask" our talents, meaning that we are seen through a haze or operate in a fog. Many years ago, camera lenses were coated to make the images less clear so that aging actors weren't seen to have so many lines and wrinkles. (Today they simply have cosmetic surgery.)

We have to face life without intervening obstacles so that our true abilities can shine clearly and vividly. Here are three conditions that we have found most mask talent and therefore most undermine mastering responsibility.

Fear

When we are fearful we tend to protect ourselves. That is a defensive posture. It may keep us safe from presumed fears, but it doesn't allow us to advance and move forward—"gain ground."

There are legitimate fears, to be sure: an approaching tornado, hereditary illness in a family, seeing someone brandish a weapon, and so forth. There are exaggerated fears: layoffs at work with no indications of them, being in a crowd and being robbed. And then there are false fears: being rejected by a prospect, being mocked when making a speech, being taken advantage of by a contractor.

When my son was young, he refused to go into the Fun House at the amusement park. "Don't be afraid of the dark," I aloofly told him.

"I'm not afraid of the dark," he countered.

"Then why won't you go in?" I asked.

"Because of what may be in the dark."

We are too often afraid of the unknown and the ambiguous and of the rumor and the innuendo. Yet, every day, many of us drive on highways at

70 miles an hour or more, with cars in front of us and in back of us that couldn't possibly stop in time in the event of an abrupt accident. We have "faith" that nothing of the sort will happen to us, though we know it does happen to others on occasion. (As I write this, there was a 130-car pileup on an icy Texas highway with several deaths.)

There are polls that claim that public speaking is a greater fear than the fear of death. Comedian Jerry Seinfeld, in a sketch standing over a coffin to deliver a eulogy, pointed out this statistic and said, "Apparently, I'm in worse shape than the guy in the box." When was the last time you saw a speaker mocked at a business meeting (let us omit university campuses)? People at meetings don't want to return and say, "What a great morning, we had a lousy speaker whom we mocked!" They want to say, "The speaker was great and I'm glad I went."

That is because people aren't "damaged" and don't live their lives by trying to hurt others (psychopaths excepted).

Most of our fears emanate from trying to protect out egos from being bruised. We "fear" rejection instead of learning from it, "fear" critique although we can accept it or reject it. Our fears are mostly inventions to protect ourselves, with the exceptions of the tornado, illness, and guns.

If you want to achieve 100 percent responsibility mastery, you must "master" your fears and understand that, in most cases, you really have nothing to fear.

Guilt

Another mask is guilt. Guilt has actually become a weapon as much as a condition. We see people "guilting" others: "Don't you realize that by using plastic bags you are ruining the environment." "Do you want to be the only one keeping us from 100 percent participation in this initiative?"

Guilt is the belief that you have committed some offense or crime or discomfort. The fact is that most of us at times *do* commit an offense or cause discomfort, intentionally or unintentionally, at times. (And if you are wondering, probably also commit a crime, because most of us exceed the speed limit at times and some of us cheat on our taxes.) Guilt is often associated with family relationships and offenses committed ages ago.

One hundred percent responsibility means:

- Accept accountability for the offense or condition.
- Apologize if appropriate and if possible.
- Learn from the error and determine how to prevent it in the future (e.g., I will not lose my temper at a meeting but talk to the individual later in private).
- Move on.

When we simply allow guilt to fester—or allow others to "guilt" us—we are enslaved. When we say apologize "if appropriate," it is hard to apologize for a slight to a classmate 30 years ago, or to a deceased relative, or a restaurant server on a vacation trip whom we will never see again. (And you don't want to try, against the odds, and then feel guilty for not having succeeded.)

The fact is we are imperfect and we make mistakes that sometimes cause others harm or discomfort. An apology should be sincere and made with the knowledge that it can't "undo" what has been done. The learning from the offense should be permanent, so that as we mature and grow, we can prevent ourselves from committing similar offenses.

But also be aware of this: Some people want to be aggrieved and offended and want you to feel guilty. A woman in a wheelchair once maneuvered herself behind me in line so that I would bump into her (I had seen her do this before at conferences). When I inevitably bumped her chairs, she said, "Oh, sure, just ignore me down here."

That's exactly what I did. Guilt is a legitimate emotion if deserved, and it can be ameliorated with the aforementioned steps. It has never been legitimated as a weapon used against someone. And the longer it lasts unattended, the more your talent will be "masked.'

Depression

I'm not talking about clinical depression here, I'm talking about feelings of despondency, loss, unacceptance, and lack of success. We *all* feel this way at times in our lives. This is a natural reaction for all of us at some times in our lives.

The way out of depressive feelings is to talk them out once you acknowledge them. It is very difficult to get through these alone, and even when that's successful it takes a huge amount of time.

Find others who are good listeners and others who may have been through the same experiences. Be vulnerable and talk through the issues. If you can't find such people, or if the issues remain nonetheless, find a good therapist.

I remember when one of my dogs died and I was morose, the first thing the therapist said was, "Tell me about your dog, and the good times you had."

As we have mentioned, we can't be therapists ourselves in terms of clinical depression. But in these kinds of "low" times, we can be that good listener and we can share our own experiences (we talk about "shared experience mastery" in Chapter 3).

We often see obvious signs of people feeling "low": low energy, lateness, lack of interest, and so forth. If we were sure that the "markers" aren't present for clinical depression, we should confront the observed behaviors and ask how we can help, suggesting things from our own experience as appropriate.

This is why trusted advisors have to take into account the "entire person," and not such the personal at work. We don't live a business life and a personal life; we just live a life.

Chapter Return on Investment

- We must adopt a zero-criticism mindset.
- We should be judgment-free and empathetic.
- We should treat ourselves and others as possessing unique gifts.
- Your self-worth is not subject to others' actions or language.
- You have to love yourself before you can love others.

- Use exercises to build your esteem daily.
- Use your own metrics, not those of others.
- ALL your experiences can be learning experiences if you allow it.
- Demonstrate your clients who was caring and vulnerable mean.
- Help others to avoid the three "masks" of talent.

CHAPTER 10

Emotional Mastery

Show up in a positive emotional state, develop mental toughness, and enjoy the trusted advisor journey moment by moment.

Achieving a Positive Emotional State

We talked earlier of "emotional health." Let us focus as we conclude this book on "emotional mastery."

Negative emotional states cost us dearly. We make bad decisions, waste time, and procrastinate. These conditions are result of feeling miserable, sad, lonely, and so forth. The result is that you dislike others, dislike your circumstances, and even dislike yourself. This dislike undermines your self-esteem, reduces your confidence, and decreases your overall confidence about your talents and prospects. The guilt, fear, and depression we discussed in the prior chapter can be caused and/or exacerbated by these emotional downers.

Emotions that lead to negativity are jealousy, envy, hatred, anger, sadness, feelings of betrayal, and lack of control.

These all are a part of our live experiences. However, they affect some people far worse than others. They shouldn't be denied but must be effectively managed. Unmanaged negative emotions can lead to excesses, even violence.

If we acknowledge them, we can control them and even turn them into positive emotions. Emotions are "real" in that what we feel is valid (see the Case Study Vignette about my son in Chapter 2). But frustration and anger, to name two, can make us uncomfortable to the point of poor performance and endangered relationships.

When you experience negative emotions, it means that something has to be changed because what is occurring at the moment is harming us. For example, anxiety indicates that we need better preparation, or more information, or more support for a future event or possibility. Fear might mean that we should increase our safety—get vaccinated or live in places where the weather is less severe.

Thus, negative emotions can be used to improve our condition.

The answer is not unbridled optimism, or "it is in God's hands," *but rather acceptance of how we are feeling and what we are feeling.* Some techniques that may be useful are as follows:

- Recognize the symptoms of a negative state and prepare to deal with them, don't ignore them or assume that they will pass.
- Don't use others' metrics. Determine how you can best deal with the emotions, don't think about how your parents did or your colleagues do.
- Get physical. Workout. Breathe. Go for walks. If you feel better physically, you can feel better emotionally.
- Forgive yourself. Don't add guilt to your burden of emotional negativity.
- Refocus on positive things you want to accomplish.
- Don't try to "reverse" the feelings. Unsupported optimism and belief that things will automatically improve can easily lead to disappointment and more negative emotions.

It is tough to alleviate negative emotions alone, and it is highly advisable that you do so with the help of trusted others. And that, of course, is where the trusted advisor comes in.

Your goal with your clients should be 90 percent of the time that they are in a positive emotional state. (This is another reason why shared experience mastery is so important, as noted earlier.) When you see signs that people are not in a positive state, you need to stop and address the issue.

Those signs may include:

- Unhappiness with all alternatives or options presented to move forward on an issue.
- "It will never work" response and mentality.
- Deferral of issues and procrastination in terms of resolutions.

- Attempts to have you, the advisor, provide all the answers rather than reacting to your client's position.
- Fatigue, shorter calls, and missed appointments.
- Unwillingness to discuss certain issues.

You need to confront these positions with the "tough love" of a great advisor. It is clear that negative emotions need special response and resolution and that in so doing, you can create very positive emotions and restore "control" to your client.

We will repeat Figure 1.2 below. Any position below the horizontal line will be one of low control and a hothouse of negative emotions.

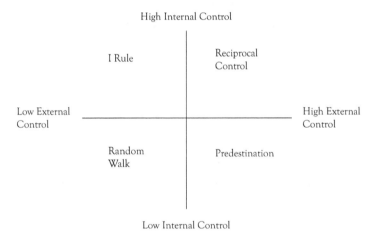

We have to be careful about "catastrophizing" the future and always assuming (and fearing) the worst. Don't allow your clients to engage in important work (evaluations, decisions, planning, priority settings, purchases, and so forth) when in a negative emotional state. You might want to increase your interactions until you can extricate them from that state.

Here are four key questions that help people escape from negative emotional states:

- Is what I believe happening true (is it valid)?
- If I'm unsure, how do I validate or invalidate it?
- How should I behave most positively at this point?
- How can I remove these thoughts?

Most of all: It is not what happens to us, it is what we do about it. Emotional mastery isn't about avoiding all negative states. It is about recognizing them and dealing with them positively.

Emotions as an Aspect of Our Decisions

Logic helps us to think, but emotions urge us to act. As advisors, we need to monitor when each is most appropriate.

For example, when we were kids, we would hear that someone called us a name or didn't want us on their team. We would feel terrible and often vengeful and attack them the next time we met. Except, that wasn't the person who called us a name, or he was the person but never called us a name, or the teams were decided by someone else, or we were on the team. The logical approach was to find out what really happened, and the emotional approach was to lash out.

The problem, as we're sure you recognize, is that as adults in business and professions, we often act the same way! We hear the boss (or the board, the customer, the employee, the supplier, or the media) has said something and we react viscerally and, usually, therefore, inappropriately under the circumstances. An emotional response is probably best when there is legitimate threat, for example, running from a fire in the building, but even there *the time to think rationally about the safest escape route might well save your life.*

Emotions are important in daily decision making, as is logic, but how much of each and under what conditions? Consider these factors:

Normative Pressure

We often call this "peer pressure," and it is an attempt to trigger an emotional response *that is in favor of the other party and only sometimes in your own.*

Have you felt the need to proceed with something you normally might not because of the actions of large numbers of others? These are not rational, logical decisions, but purely emotional ones.

There is something I will call the "threshold principle" that means that your normal, probable reactions are overcome one a threshold of others'

Case Study Vignette

At Prudential Insurance, where I obtained my first job, employees responsible for a campaign (blood drive, charity contributions, and so forth) would visit to solicit our participation. If we declined or asked for time to consider, we would be told, "Are you really prepared to be the *only* one who prevents us from 100 percent participation? Do you know what that would mean for the division when the results are published?"

We usually caved in to such pressure.

actions become apparent. A perfectly upstanding citizen, in the midst of a riot in the streets, might steal something from a shattered store window because everyone around is doing so, and it becomes a temporary "norm" endorsed by peers. A brave soldier might run if all around are, but, conversely, a scared soldier who might stay if all around are staying.

I have seen otherwise fine people cheat on expense reports, or client promises, or steal supplies because everyone else is. You tend to find corruption in police forces when there is a history of it. The acts don't have to be "endorsed," but they just need to go unpunished.

We need to help our clients to resist purely peer pressures. How many people tried to follow the late Tony Hsieh's "holocracy" management style, which is totally ineffective for almost all other companies[1] because it was deemed "trendy" and written up in the media?

Remember these:

- Open book management
- Management by wandering around
- Good to great
- Open meetings
- Reengineering

---

[1] And caused his own company to lose about 25 percent of employees via resignation.

A consultant and I both working at Hewlett Packard for many years became concerned every time our mutual client went off to another seminar, worried about what new "flavor of the month" she would now want to implement!

The Chess Game

The opposite end of this spectrum is the highly rational and analytic evaluations of all factors devoid of emotion. Grand masters in chess can think 20 moves ahead. That is why competitive chess uses timers, because otherwise the games could take days.

We have encountered people who want facts, figures, numbers, validation, verification, references, and color-coded reports. But this extreme leads to the fabled "paralysis by analysis." There is *never* enough information and enough data. Perfection undermines excellence, and assurances block action.

Emotion creates the need to act, which is why it is so vital in sales and in persuasion in general. One of the greatest links to emotion is *scarcity*; the feeling and belief are that if you don't act now, it will be "too late."

And so we hear:

- Today only
- Order now
- Offer ends tomorrow
- By midnight tonight
- Holiday special
- While supplies last

These are purely emotional triggers. If we thought about it, we would realize that the "going out of business" sign on the storefront has been there for over a year or that the special weekend discount is every weekend.

Either of these extremes of acute emotional reaction and overanalytic precision will result in generally poor decisions. If you watch a great quarterback like Tom Brady, who is being rushed and threatened with pain if

---

Case Study Vignette

I was in yet another hotel room in a different time zone awaiting my speech the next day, and I couldn't sleep. I was surfing the channels when I came across an infomercial for a "thumb wrench." I couldn't imagine what a thumb wrench was, so I watched.

This device, braced on your thumb, could create leverage for a variety of jobs. It seemed to me that any number of any other tools could do these things equally well or better. However, a clock in the corner of the screen was counting down to midnight, and there were six minutes left. The announcer informed us that we could get two thumb wrenches for the price of one (plus extra shipping charges, of course) but only if we ordered by midnight.

As I watched the clock tick down to 90 seconds, I called and provided my credit card. As a result, I have two thumb wrenches on my workbench today, never having used either and completely unaware of how they can be used. There are no instructions.

---

tackled so that there is an urgency to throw the ball, you will see that he is also rationally looking downfield at four potential receivers and deciding on who makes the most sense for a successful play.

When I have observed, very successful managers interview candidates using criteria and sound judgment; they have several candidates who are very close to ideal to choose from, and they then tend to "go with their gut" (which is what I advise them to do at that point).

Thus, it is a combination of ensuring that you are using all the facts at your disposal combined with a sense of urgency to take action, each counter-balancing the other.

Finding Cause

Your clients will often seek blame instead of cause, sometimes without even realizing it. We tend to want to know *who* is responsible for a setback, a missed deadline, a poor quality product, or service. The implication is that someone has advertently or inadvertently hurt us.

Case Study Vignette

When I have asked excellent leaders how they make their decisions, about 20 percent have said, "It is just natural and internal, I can't describe it."

This is an untruth.

They either have a process they choose not to explain, or they have one that they really can't articulate. In either case, I have walked them through it, and it turned out they had a methodical way to both analyze and take action. In other words, content and speed were both important.

When I was the president of a behavioral consulting firm, I asked out consulting psychologist, Peter, how he interpreted psychometric test results. "I just look at the *gestalt*," he told me. "Yes," I said, "but take me though each step you use." I found his process very easily, and it combined his observation of the data and his experience with such data to form information and knowledge about the subject.

To be crude but honest, this is "scapegoating." Let us find someone to blame so that we can get on with our business. However, once you assign blame you haven't solved the problem or improved performance. The lousy result is still sitting there and probably causing lingering effects.

Have you ever made an unavoidable mistake? Or when you have made an avoidable mistake was it a learning experience that made you better in the long run? Life is about success, not perfection, after all.

Consultants often walk into a client's office and assume that it is the client who is the problem! The very person "smart enough" to have hired them is at the same time "dumb enough" to have caused the problem and not even know it. This is the same phenomenon as scapegoating. I call it, "assuming the other person is damaged."

In your advisory work, don't make such assumptions and don't allow your clients to do so, either. These are emotional leaps that must be prevented. The urgency seems to be "jump to cause (blame)" so that the problems can be quickly "solved," though the truth is that this actually prolongs their being unsolved!

In these cases, we have to move from emotionalism to rationalism, which is an important aspect of emotional mastery. A problem exists because:

- There is a deviation from what is expected to performance less than expected.
- Cause is unknown.
- We care.

If we don't care, there's no sense trying to do anything. I don't care if the garage door has begun squeaking a bit. If we know cause, then we have a decision to make, not a problem to solve. The cause is the dry springs, and I can lubricate them. And if there is no deviation, then why am I concerned? If the garage doors aren't squeaking, there is nothing for me to do right now. (If I'm concerned about them squeaking in the future, then that is a plan to implement with some preventive maintenance twice a year that I will put on my calendar.)

Emotional mastery is the age-old adage about knowing when to hold and when to fold. That is, we need to appreciate when we need emotion and urgency and when we need rationality and careful consideration. Of course, sometimes we need both.

That means we ask, "How did this happened," and not, "Who did this?"

Creating the Emotional/Rational Mix

There are two equally dangerous extremes: to be totally emotional and to be totally rational. That might shock you.

We pointed out that even in calamity and chaos—fire, tornado, gunshots—while emotion generates flight, we have to make rational decisions about our best routes and courses of action. And even when we've carefully analyzed every detail of new candidates for a key position, we need our visceral responses to whom we most would like to hire. (I recall a cartoon with a job interviewer and a candidate across the desk from each other, and they looked exactly alike. The interviewer says, "I don't know what it is, but I just like you!" Of course, that's NOT the way to hire!)

Case Study Vignette

My father enlisted in the first paratroop regiment ever formed in the U.S. Army just before World War II. It was all volunteer, and he wound up jumping into enemy guns in New Guinea defending Australia against invasion. He died one month shy of 100 years old of natural causes.

When I was young, he talked me into going with him on the old Parachute Jump ride at Coney Island in New York. It was frightening, and I was terrified. People on the beach looked like ants. And at the top, you were released and descended by a parachute (but controlled by cables). It was, of course, closed in a more safety-minded age, but the old structure was till there last time I visited.

However, after that I began riding on giant roller coasters for the first time, having completely overcome my fear after rationally concluding that if I could stand the Parachute Jump, I could certainly ride the roller coasters. And I did—from the first seat in the front car.

The best leaders combine these traits. So do we all as we mature.

Many people fear, viscerally, public speaking (largely because they are told to by others who fear it). Yet once they successfully do it, they grow to love it. The rationality is that people in the audience are there to support you, not undermine you. After that, it is a pleasure.

Our tendency toward change and disruption has often been described as "fight or flight" by the psychologists, but let us add "fright" to that dynamic.

Flight Fight Fright

When that proverbial deer is frozen in the headlights, it can't fight the menace, but it can flee and often does. However, when it doesn't, it is because it is too frightened to move. And many of us are often too frightened to move. So we don't make the business decision claiming we need more information or assurances even though there are no more to be had. We fear raising an issue with our spouse or partner even though it is causing us pain.

There is what I call a "pain pivot." That is the point at which we can take action and endure some short-term pain that will eliminate longer term pain, or we can refuse to take action and continue to bear pain forever. We are afraid of the pain of telling a family member that they can't be successful in the business, so we endure their poor performance. We are afraid of the discomfort of telling a colleague that they have bad breath, so we hold out breath during unavoidable car rides. We can't withstand the pain (embarrassment) of telling friends that we can't join them at an expensive restaurant or on a vacation, so we prolong the financial pain of spending money we don't have and borrowing at high interest rates.

In business, with the people you advise, you will encounter:

Flight

People will run from trouble or pain. They will ask someone else to deliver the bad news in an evaluation or a staff meeting. They will refuse to hear customer feedback or complaints. They won't deal with the supplier with whom they were 90 days overdue on payments. They will make excuses not to appear at a board meeting. They will consistently cancel appointments with you, fearing bad feedback or not having met their own accountabilities.

When people have made public accountabilities (I will lose 10 pounds, I will have the new product available on May 1) they are even more prone to "flee" if the commitment will be missed.

Fight

You will have pugnacious clients whose first call will be to the legal department! They will retaliate against customers or employees rather than endure argument and negative feedback. These clients will often have excuses for themselves and tell you that your expectations are unreasonable or methods are ineffective.

Because of this tendency to fight, they will be approached less often and they will believe their tactic works. But, in reality, people will just circumvent them and never tell them the truth. The way to face down a

Case Study Vignette

I had coached a client, Belinda, on how to find the ideal buyer for her services, how to engage that person and create trust, and then how to pivot to a proposal and an offer of help.

She and I found that it was because she was contenting herself to talk to low level, nonthreatening people instead of doing the work to be introduced to the real buyer. But she blamed me.

"Your approach doesn't work. The people I talk to don't want to receive a proposal. I have been consistently unsuccessful."

"That's because you are not doing what I have advised, and you are not talking to buyers."

"That is not it, your methods aren't effective."

"Then why do they work for everyone else and not you? Why am I successful advising people in this manner and only you can't seem to make it work? Is the distinction you or me?"

We parted company. You can't help people who don't want to be helped and who want to fight about it.

---

bully is to confront them, because bullyism is the result of an inferiority complex there, the bully tries to bring others down to his or her own perceived level of mediocrity.

Fright

This is the toughest because it is not readily revealed in many cases. It is insidious because it is not as obvious as fleeing or fighting. People can go to great lengths to camouflage their fears. Explaining that you have a prior appointment and can't go dancing is also a way to avoid fears of embarrassment on the dance floor. Graciously allowing a colleague to make the recommendations to the board can also indicate you don't have the courage to do it yourself.

We have to overcome our fears, which too often originate in trying to protect out ego. After all, the fear of being critique for procrastinating is more bearable to many people than the fear of being critiqued for the poor quality of the finished product.

Many of our fears are subliminal. They are based on something our parents told us, or our friends reinforced, or the norms of the culture. Once upon a time you couldn't go in the water for an hour after eating or you would get cramps and drown! We would count down the final 60 seconds and plunge in. Today, we know that's ridiculous. We were told that most people are afraid of public speaking, so we think we should be, too.

Consequently, we have to dispel our own mythologies and seek the empirical truths. (Remember when red meat was going to kill us?)

The overt fears must be faced down. If we are going to be audited by the IRS, then get a professional accountant to represent you and get your records in order. If you are concerned about flying, get therapy (which usually involved taking short hops first for acclimation). If you fear driving in the snow, don't do it. There are alternatives.

Thus, we have to conquer our fears to gain emotional mastery and help our clients overcome theirs for the same reasons. Imagine if you feared giving advice!?

Chapter Return on Investment

- We waste our time and make poor decisions in negative emotional states.
- We must "show up" positive.
- Ask what success looks like for you.
- Ask what it is you really want to achieve.
- Ask what is your purpose (who do you want to be)?
- Anger, guilt, and fear will "mask" your talent. The same for others.
- Keep a "gratitude journal." Remind yourself of what you want to accomplish each morning, and what you have accomplished each evening, personal or professional, large or small.

- Use fight, flight, fright positively, and point out to your clients how to avoid them and how best to deal with them when unavoidable.
- Fears are overt and covert and equally undermining.
- To overcome fear is to create a masterful emotional state, which support positive attitudes and successful decisions.

Epilog

We have attempted to provide you with our best practices for being a valuable and sought-after trusted advisor. Some of your effectiveness will depend on your talent, of course, but more of it will rely on your discipline, focus, generosity, and empathy.

In others words, these are learned behaviors and developed skills.

Our practical experience is significant. Thus, this book has not been theoretical but pragmatic. Nancy has created a trusted advisor "boot camp" of sorts called Inspired Leadership—You Go First. People learn and apply during this experience the 10 mastery factors for success.

I practice two techniques that solidify my success:

- The Oxygen Mask Principle: This, of course, maintains that you must take care of yourself first before you can help others. Hence, we're emphasized with your own health, ego control, emotional mastery, and so forth before you can help others to apply these techniques to themselves.
- The One Percent Solution®: If you improve by just 1 percent a day, in 70 days you'll be twice as good! (If you don't believe that, try it on your calculator.) Yet not enough people improve by 1 percent a day because they are just repeating what they did yesterday. Master one of these techniques—or even a part of one—daily or weekly, and you'll become expert. Don't try to apply them all at once, and the same holds true for your clients.

In fact, it is a lifetime journey as conditions change and we all keep growing. Surround yourself with peers and your own trusted advisors who believe in this philosophy and who can help you to grow. This can exponentially increase your learning and effectiveness of application. Use the exercises you learn here (e.g., three positives morning and evening, or generalize success but isolate failures) and that you may learn elsewhere.

And practice these techniques in your daily life. Show up judgment-free and with zero criticism at the outset. One of the reasons our society is so polarized—and companies can divide into "warring camps" and silos—is that people interact with judgments and criticism store up and eager to explode. To facilitate your judgment-free position, demonstrate vulnerability not defensiveness and demonstrate empathy not merely sympathy.

Perhaps the most difficult part for some of you will be loving yourself—if you stop judging yourself, then it will be harder to judge others. After all, if we were to merely compare ourselves to friends, colleagues, classmates, we wouldn't feel too badly about ourselves! We would tend to be "average" in looks, talents, abilities, and so forth. But every day we are besieged with advertising, entertainment, social media, and other sources that throw in our faces the most beautiful people, the most affluent people, and the most athletic people.

Those are terrible daily comparisons to have to lug around, and many of those "stellar" examples are, themselves, miserable. Actors, for example, are terribly insecure, and most of them holding awards after a ceremony honoring them are actually wondering if they will ever work again!

Advise your clients not to compare themselves to others, not to judge themselves that way, and therefore not judge their employees, peers, or superiors.

Of course, we all make "judgments": Was the vacation fulfilling, was the meal cooked properly, whom should be invite to the party? We are confident that you can see the difference between making evaluations based on our experiences, and operating with a *tabla rasa* (a "clean slate") when it comes to our daily interactions with others, whether friends, colleagues, or strangers.

As trusted advisors, we have a huge role, even accountability, in eliminating bias. That includes sexism, ageism, racism, biases about abilities, and denial of opportunity. The key here is that many of these destructive biases are "hidden" or subconscious, even though they manifest themselves in the workplace and in society.

If we create zero-criticism, judgment-free mentalities, we help people to deal with everyone on an equal basis.

Case Study Vignette

A client of mine, Jane, who is Chinese by origin but is third-genera-tion American offered to enable our small coaching group to obtain a great table in the best Chinese restaurant in the city. I had never even been able to get to the second floor that had the best seating before this.

Over drinks, the waiter came around and I said to her, "Please tell him that I will start with the crab."

She said to the waiter, "He will have the crab."

I said to her, "Why did you tell him in English?"

She said, "What makes you think I can speak Chinese?"

I had known her for five years.

A great deal of the bias we encounter is "hidden" in the respect that we make assumptions no grounded in reality, not factual, not observed. I became acutely aware of that through as assumption that a woman who was of Chinese origin and often talked about her grandparents' progress in this country would naturally speak Chinese.

This raised the issue of what more serious hidden biases we possess of which we were unaware, het act on them anyway. When I did the baseline study on diversity for a company in the Fortune top 20, here is what I found *told to me* in interviews and focus groups by employees at various levels:

- I was told that I would never be promoted beyond my current positions because of my accented English.
- Asians are great researchers, but they can't confront people, so they can't be promoted into senior management ranks.
- Our CFO, a woman, is an exception at that rank, and she had to choose not to have a family in order to attain that rank.
- "We have to exclusionary practices of 'tribes' here," a senior executive told me, and then I showed him the lunchtime cafeteria where people were sitting by color, by ethnicity, even by gender.

- The racial minorities, even those considered to be senior management, were disproportionately place in human resources, legal, finance, and support service, rather than sales, manufacturing, operations, and line functions.
- All the board members were white males.

If you review our 10 mastery areas, they are overlapping and mutually reinforcing. ego mastery and emotional mastery are reciprocal, for example. While you can proceed in a methodical manner and don't need to move forward on all fronts immediately, you should cover all of the areas eventually. And you have to set the example for that to happen. *You* have to walk the talk first.

Nancy has long believed that her calling is to fill the world with inspiring leaders, and so she has created small groups of executives and business owners globally who meet regularly—and virtually—under the guidance of a chairperson who is a trusted advisor, both with the group and as part of their own consulting and coaching practices. The overwhelming evidence from these groups is that these leaders are most effective when they are caring, vulnerable, and assertive people. That is, they are showing up "as the best version of themselves."

All of us, on occasion, need help and guidance that we are not "imposters," that we are worthy, talented, and intelligent. We need to eschew the media comparisons to the most beautiful, athletic, talented, and wealthiest people in the world and use our own, more relevant and meaningful metrics.

As modern trusted advisors, we need to see ourselves and treat ourselves as peers of our clients, fellow human beings all on this journey of life together, trying to make the greatest contribution to others that we can make every day, because helping them helps us.

Leaders are lonelier than ever today. Sometimes you may feel lonely too. Let us hope that this book has helped you to focus on becoming the best version of yourself every single day, so that you can help others to do so, as well.

"First do no harm" may be the medical creed, but we prefer the words of George Merck, who founded a pharmaceutical giant with a vision of bringing the greatest in scientific research to the greatest areas of human health needs:

"Do good, and good will follow."

About the Authors

Dr. Nancy MacKay is the founder and CEO of MacKay CEO Forums, the highest impact and least time intensive peer group for more than 1,200 CEOs, Executives, and business owners around the world. With a dream to populate the world with inspiring leaders, she founded MacKay CEO Forums in 2005; after seeing firsthand, the tremendous value of having CEOs come together to learn from each other, and to help each other deal with their toughest issues and challenges.

More than 60 Forum Chairs, who are all very successful trusted advisors, facilitate more than 100 peer learning groups, involving more than 700 meetings and retreats each year. As a Certified B. Corp, MacKay CEO Forums is committed to using business as a force for good in the world.

Nancy is a CEO coach, Forum Chair, dynamic keynote speaker, published author, and a former university professor.

She is the host of the weekly MacKay CEO Forums EDGE events with thousands of CEO, Executive, and Business Owner participants from around the world. Nancy holds a B.Math and a Master's degree in Management Sciences from the University of Waterloo, as well as a PhD in Business from Canterbury University in New Zealand.

She is the coauthor with Alan Weiss of *The Talent Advantage* by Wiley Publishing. Based on her coaching work with hundreds of CEOs, she has authored the "MacKay Mastery Model for Inspired Leadership—You Go First Strategy", a guide, a roadmap for business leaders to inspire themselves every day to take positive action.

Nancy lives in BC, Canada. She loves to play squash, and, over the past decade, she has travelled to more than 33 countries around the world with her family.

Nancy is on the advisory board of Blueprint, which is a catalyst in the conversation of men in the world to help men be a force for equity, compassion, and sustainability.

Alan Weiss is one of those rare people who can say he is a consultant, speaker, and author, and I mean it. His consulting firm, Summit Consulting Group, Inc., has attracted clients such as Merck, Hewlett-Packard, GE, Mercedes-Benz, State Street Corporation, Times Mirror Group, The Federal Reserve, The New York Times Corporation, and more than 400 other leading organizations.

He has served on the board of directors of the Trinity Repertory Company, a Tony-Award-winning New England regional theater, chaired Newport International Film Festival board of trustees, Festival Ballet Providence where he is currently president of the board, and the Harvard Center for Mental Health and the Media.

His speaking typically includes 30 keynotes a year at major conferences, and he has been a visiting faculty member at Case Western Reserve University, Boston College, Tufts, St. John's, the University of Illinois, the Institute of Management Studies, and the University of Georgia Graduate School of Business. He has held an appointment as adjunct professor in the Graduate School of Business at the University of Rhode Island where he taught courses on advanced management and consulting skills. He holds the record for selling out the highest priced workshop (on entrepreneurialism) in the 21-year history of New York City's Learning Annex. His PhD is in psychology.

He is an inductee into the Professional Speaking Hall of Fame® and the concurrent recipient of the National Speakers Association Council of Peers Award of Excellence, representing the top 1 percent of professional speakers in the world. He is a Fellow of the Institute of Management Consultants, one of only two people in the world holding both honors.

His prolific publishing includes more than 500 articles and 60 books, including his best-seller, *Million Dollar Consulting* (in its sixth edition from McGraw-Hill). His latest is *Your Legacy Is Now (2021)*. His books have been on the curricula at Villanova, Temple University, UC Berkeley, and the Wharton School of Business, and have been translated into 15 languages. The Wharton School used his first book, *The Innovation Formula*, in its graduate programs.

He is interviewed and quoted frequently in the media, and his career has taken him to 61 countries and 49 states. (He is afraid to go to North Dakota.) *Success Magazine* has cited him in an editorial devoted to his work as "a worldwide expert in executive education." The *New York Post* calls him "one of the most highly regarded independent consultants in America." He is the winner of the prestigious Axiem Award for Excellence in Audio Presentation.

He has received the Lifetime Achievement Award of the American Press Institute, the first-ever for a nonjournalist, and one of only seven awarded in the 60-year history of the association.

He once appeared on the popular American TV game show *Jeopardy*, where he lost badly in the first round to a dancing waiter from Iowa. He lives in East Greenwich, RI, with his wife of 53 years Maria, and his dogs Coco and Bentley, a white German Shepherd who also stars in one of his video series, "The Writing on the Wall."

Index

OTHER TITLES IN THE HUMAN RESOURCE MANAGEMENT AND ORGANIZATIONAL BEHAVIOR COLLECTION

Michael Provitera, Barry University, Editor

- *A.I. and Remote Working* by Tony Miller
- *Best Boss!* by Duncan Ferguson, Toni M. Pristo, and John Furcon
- *Managing for Accountability* by Lynne Curry
- *Emotional Connection: The EmC Strategy* by Lola Gershfeld and Ramin Sedehi
- *Fundamentals of Level Three Leadership* by James G.S. Clawson
- *Civility at Work* by Lewena Bayer
- *Lean on Civility* by Christian Masotti and Lewena Bayer
- *The Successful New CEO* by Christian Muntean
- *Agility* by Michael Edmondson
- *Strengths Oriented Leadership* by Matt L. Beadle
- *Leadership in Disruptive Times* by Sattar Bawany
- *The Truth About Collaborating* by Dr. Gail Levitt
- *Level-Up Leadership* by Michael J. Provitera
- *Uses and Risks of Business Chatbots* by Tania Peitzker
- *Three Key Success Factors for Transforming Your Business* by Michael Hagemann

Concise and Applied Business Books

The Collection listed above is one of 30 business subject collections that Business Expert Press has grown to make BEP a premiere publisher of print and digital books. Our concise and applied books are for...

- Professionals and Practitioners
- Faculty who adopt our books for courses
- Librarians who know that BEP's Digital Libraries are a unique way to offer students ebooks to download, not restricted with any digital rights management
- Executive Training Course Leaders
- Business Seminar Organizers

Business Expert Press books are for anyone who needs to dig deeper on business ideas, goals, and solutions to everyday problems. Whether one print book, one ebook, or buying a digital library of 110 ebooks, we remain the affordable and smart way to be business smart. For more information, please visit www.businessexpertpress.com, or contact sales@businessexpertpress.com.

CPSIA information can be obtained
at www.ICGtesting.com
Printed in the USA
BVHW042151261021
620002BV00013B/526

9 781637 421376